Penguin Special

The Break-up of the Soviet Empire in
Eastern Europe

Ghita Ionescu was born in Bucharest in 1913.
After university he served as Rumanian Economic
Counsellor in Bulgaria and Turkey and at the end
of the war, as a high official of the Armistice
Commission, he took part in negotiations with the
Soviet representatives in Rumania. In 1946 he
resigned from the Rumanian Diplomatic Service
and came to live in England the following year.
He is now a Nuffield Fellow in Eastern European
politics at the London School of Economics and
Political Science.

Ghita Ionescu has specialized in economic and
political studies on Eastern Europe, and his book,
Communism in Rumania, 1944–1962, is recognized
as an authoritative work on the subject. He is now
engaged on further studies of modern political
systems.

The Break-up
of the Soviet Empire in
Eastern Europe

Ghita Ionescu

Penguin Books

Penguin Books Ltd, Harmondsworth, Middlesex, England
Penguin Books Inc, 7110 Ambassador Road, Baltimore, Md. 21207, U.S.A.
Penguin Books Australia Ltd, Ringwood, Victoria, Australia

First published 1965 by Penguin Books Ltd
Published 1969 by Penguin Books Inc
SBN 14 052243 3

Printed in the United States of America by Publication Press

Contents

To Professor Philip E. Mosely
from whom I have learned so much

Introduction

Twenty years have passed since five Eastern European countries – Poland, Rumania, Bulgaria, Hungary, Czechoslovakia – and part of another country, Eastern Germany, were included in Soviet Russia's zone of domination in Europe, and they have been ruled ever since by Communist Governments. Two other countries, Yugoslavia and Albania, are also governed by Communists, but do not form part of Russia's zone of domination.

Twenty years, by any standards, is a sizeable span of time; it amounts to the passing of a generation. It is a period which has shown us that with the help of the technical and political means at present available, dictatorial parties can establish and maintain themselves comfortably in power, as they have in Soviet Russia and in the two Iberian countries. What were the circumstances in which these governments were established in Eastern Europe? Has this continuity, regardless of the means by which it has been achieved, been a significant factor in the evolution of these countries? Has it been long enough and powerful enough to mould these peoples so as to orientate, or, to use a more Marxist expression, to *determine* their future evolution? And has what is called in this book the Soviet Empire in Eastern Europe been able to resist the disruptive forces of the last twenty years, or on the contrary disintegrated under their pressure, and how, and why?

The expression 'empire' is not used here in a metaphorical sense. An empire is characterized by three basic elements. The first is the existence of a strong political centre, animated by a historical mission of expansion. The second is the element of religious or ideological coercion used to weld it into a single coordinated or expanding unit. The third is a sense of final purpose justifying it and inspiring its officers, soldiers and officials to transcend their individual role in the particular phase of development in which they find themselves.

In the case of Stalin's Russia the three elements can be clearly seen. The strong centre of direction was ultimately the Politburo and/or Secretariat of the Communist Party of the Soviet Union (henceforth referred to by its initials CPSU) with Stalin at its head. (The almost simultaneous foundation of the USSR and of the Communist International, the supreme Communist organ in the rest of the world, but dependent on the CPSU, enabled Stalin to fuse those historical growths and to pervert them completely to his own ends. His private ambition to dominate the world combined with his very different public statements of his historical mission to give the advance of Russian communism from 1920 to 1960 its distinctive character.)

The element of coercion was provided by the party (controlling the other parties as well), the MVD (the secret police) and the Soviet army, vital to the establishment of communism outside Soviet Russia.

Finally, the belief or mystique was provided by the Marxist–Leninist–Stalinist ideology – a strange mixture of the old Communist inspiration adapted to the realities of Soviet rule – though this suffered from the basic illogicality of asserting both Russian hegemony and the equality of all Communist parties, countries and governments.

Chapter 1 of this book covers briefly the period of the building of Stalin's empire, which divides itself into two main phases: 1943–7, in which the establishment of the military zone of imperial domination of Soviet Russia in Europe took place, and 1947–54, which saw the forceful attempt by Stalin to transform this zone into a proper contemporary empire, with all the political, administrative, economic, ideological and even personal elements of an empire clearly stressed and made to function together under a central force and a widely ramified network of coercion.

The rest of this survey considers the break-up of Stalin's empire after Stalin's death at the hands of Khrushchev and those who follow him. This break-up can be traced in the three successive losses of authority of the CPSU, each the result of a rebellion within the Communist bloc. First came that of the revisionists or national Communists (Chapter 2); then that of the dogmatists (Chapter 3); and lastly that of the neutralists (Chapter 4). Although they had different and indeed opposed aims, these three rebellions had and have in common one thing: their determination to put an end to the domination and control of the CPSU. And together they form, from a historical point of view, the story of the decline and fall of Stalin's empire.

In conclusion I have tried to sum up present trends and developments, and to give an indication of what one might expect to happen in the future.

The reader who would like to know more about the history of Eastern Europe and its intrinsic importance in European and world history will find a brief account in the Appendix, followed by a selected bibliography on the subject.

1 The Building of the Empire (1944-8)

(i) The watershed: Teheran and after

Like Lenin, and indeed like any genuine Bolshevik, Stalin was a voluntarist, that is a revolutionary who, although he believes in some historically determined conditions for political and social changes, knows that they have to be effected by direct, or even violent action. But more than Lenin, he believed in force as the only reliable means of action. While Lenin might have found some room in his assessment of a given situation for such imponderabilia as the people's needs, moods and claims, Stalin believed that these and other factors did not contribute essentially to the shaping of the situation, and in any case could be altered by the firm use of force. From this point of view his 'socialism in one country' was a policy of bringing into shape new social and political realities exclusively and directly by the means in one's possession. Force was the lever and was also the yardstick. In every situation pressure should be brought to bear; but in no situation should one go farther than the limit of one's force, however promising and encouraging the reactions one could count on from friendly quarters.

In terms of strategy, political, diplomatic or military, this implied a preference for bases and jumping-off boards as near as possible to any potential trouble spot; for the sharpest and most effective tools for action; and for as overwhelming a superiority in forces, actual and potential, as could be built up before the action. Thus, as far as the instruments were concerned, Stalin preferred for his internal policies the secret police to the party and for external ones the Soviet army (and the external ramifications of the NKVD) to the foreign Communist parties or the Communist International. As far as the bases were concerned, territorial contiguity and defensive depth were what he aimed at. In 1940, he had obtained the Baltic States, the eastern part of

Poland and Bessarabia. He surely thought of them as 'marches' and 'buffer-zones'. But he assimilated them, territorially, politically and ideologically, into the USSR in an unmistakably imperialistic way. When in 1943 the war was drawing to an end, he was already considering, with an audacious sense of historical timing, his future relations with those countries which, after the Reich's collapse, would be the neighbouring powers 'somewhere in Europe'.

For those in search of the starting-point of the Cold War, or indeed of European and Eastern European post-war history, the Teheran Conference of 27 November to 3 December 1943 is, in retrospect, the watershed. (The recent publication by the US State Department of the basic documents of the conference has also helped towards a better understanding of its importance.*) It already had its place in history as the first conference at which Churchill, Roosevelt and Stalin met together. Now it can be seen as the conference at which the fateful decision was taken, before the final attack on Europe, which was Hitler's fortress, to divide it into two exclusive zones of operation, with the Anglo-American forces in the West and the Soviet army in the East. In the minds of the Western Governments this was, of course, only a provisional military agreement; and not only did Stalin treat it again and again in his speeches as such but indeed the conference also issued declarations stressing the international harmony and justice upon which the future post-war collaboration of the Powers was to be based. But in Stalin's eyes this was the beginning of a new revolutionary advance by Russia. He came already prepared with the idea and had an easy game to play against the British and the Americans, who were unaware of his intentions and were not fully in agreement with each other on this particular issue of how to launch the offensive in Europe.

What happened was that before the conference met the American and the British Chiefs of Staff had prepared separate documents expressing somewhat different points of view about

* US Department of State: *The Conference of Cairo and Teheran, 1943* (Washington, 1961).

the new phase for which they were preparing in 1942–3: the invasion of Europe. Already from previous exchanges of views, at other conferences, or even in correspondence, it had become evident that the American Chiefs of Staff were growing impatient with the slower timetable proposed by the British. They also disliked the insistent British suggestion that more than one front should be opened on the Continent, considering this to be an unnecessary waste of energy and dispersal of forces. Britain proposed that one of these fronts should be opened somewhere in the Balkans, whence, with Turkey's help, the Anglo–American forces could outflank the large part of the German war-machine which was still engaged in that zone, and then join the Soviet army at some point in south-east Europe. The Americans, with their enormous striking force and potential and their untapped resources, preferred the idea of a single major and decisive strategic blow (an idea which was also more congenial to their general outlook and methods of action) to the dispersed and slow-moving British policy, which would delay the operation and disperse the forces needed for it.

As the date of the Teheran Conference and of the first tripartite confrontation of plans was drawing closer, the American Chiefs of Staff in a 'Statement of United States Strategic Policy in the Balkan–Eastern Mediterranean Region' made very clear their view that operations in the Balkan–Aegean area should be limited to the supplying of Balkan guerrillas by sea and air, minor action by Commando forces and the bombing of vital strategic targets. The documents were sent to the British, but no conclusion was agreed on before the meeting with the Russians.

In the first phase of the conference the British, that is Churchill and Alanbrooke, are on record as insisting that in any case some Allied forces should be held in reserve for operations in the Balkans. On 28 November Churchill emphasized that Turkey's entry into the war would have a great effect upon Rumania and Hungary, and might well start a landslide among the satellite states. He suggested that Soviet Russia herself might be sufficiently interested in the operation to agree to a two or three months' delay in the launching of Overlord (the invasion of Europe across the Channel) for this purpose. Roosevelt said that 'he had thought of a possible operation at the head of the Adriatic to make a junction with the partisans under Tito and then to operate north-east into Rumania in conjunction with the Soviet advance from the region of Odessa'.

Stalin, however, having listened to all these points and tentative suggestions, came down strongly against any 'dissipation' of the Anglo–American forces in the Mediterranean and in favour of the launching of Overlord at the earliest possible moment. In the 'military agreement' of 1 December 1943 the three leaders agreed on the following five crucial points: (1) to support Tito's partisans in Yugoslavia with supplies and by Commando operations; (2) to welcome the possibility of Turkey's entry into the war (which became a forlorn hope only a fortnight later when at the Cairo Conference the Turks found that they were not sufficiently encouraged to take the final plunge); (3) to provide for Russia's entry into war with Bulgaria should Bulgaria attack Turkey; (4) to launch Overlord in May 1944, when the Soviet forces would also launch a massive offensive; and (5) to keep in close touch with each other with regard to the impending operations in Europe.

Once it had thus been decided that the two forces, the Anglo–American on one side and the Soviet on the other, would advance from the two opposite ends of the Continent towards a point in the centre of Europe, where they could meet according to procedures and delimitations to be worked out later, there was little doubt that the entirely free hand won by Stalin for the Soviet army in half the continent would entail some weighty political consequences. The Communist Parties of Eastern Europe realized this immediately and prepared for action. This is how the Teheran Conference came to be, from the beginning, the decisive one.

Much more ink has been spilt on the subject of the Yalta Conference of 4–11 February 1945, which is considered by many statesmen, historians and journalists as Stalin's greatest diplomatic *coup* against the naïve British and Americans. Yet it can be seen in retrospect that there was an attempt at the Yalta

Conference (at which some mistakes were undoubtedly made, as for instance the inclusion in the Soviet zone of influence of North Korea up to the 38th parallel) to redress some of the harm done in Teheran and before. Thus the Yalta Conference was the first, even if belated, occasion on which the United States showed a direct interest in Central and Eastern European affairs. Until then the American Chiefs of Staff had most categorically forbidden any commitments of American power in Europe beyond Germany (even Austria was at first included in the 'Balkan zone') or in the Mediterranean.

The platonic agreements worked out at Yalta for some compromise on the Governments in Poland and the other Eastern European countries could not of course change the *de facto* situation already created by the fact that the Soviet army was the sole master and arbiter of the region; but it put forward some principles which, vague though they were, nevertheless had to be trampled upon later by Stalin. From this particular point of view, Yalta was an attempt to improve, on paper at least, the situation already created by the fact that from 1944 the Soviet Union, because of the massive presence of Soviet troops, was able to play a direct and decisive part in the internal politics of every country in Eastern Europe.

The same is true also of the celebrated Stalin–Churchill agreement of October 1944, which many historians consider to be the decisive moment when Eastern Europe was lost to Russia. The agreement, one must admit, is far from being morally commendable. Churchill himself describes it in his *Second World War* in sober terms, when he speaks of the visit he and Eden paid to Moscow in October 1944:

The moment was apt for business, so I said, 'Let us settle about our affairs in the Balkans. Your armies are in Rumania and Bulgaria. We have interests, missions and agents there. Don't let us get at cross-purposes in small ways. So far as Britain and Russia are concerned, how would it do for you to have ninety per cent predominance in Rumania, for us to have ninety per cent of the say in Greece, and go fifty-fifty in Yugoslavia?' While this was being translated, I wrote out on a half-sheet of paper:

Rumania: Russia 90%, others 10%

Greece: Great Britain (in accord with USA) 90%, Russia 10%
Yugoslavia: 50–50%
Hungary: 50–50%
Bulgaria: Russia 75%, the others 25%.

I pushed this across to Stalin, who had by then heard the translation. There was a slight pause. Then he took his blue pencil and made a large tick upon it and passed it back to us. It was all settled in no more time than it takes to set it down.

Yet the fact remains that if there was going to be a bargain on such a basis, it was in Britain's favour – for while the Soviet armies were already in Rumania and in the other Eastern European countries, where they could with impunity do what they wished, they were not in Greece and could by this move be excluded from it. But, apart from the fact that for this and many other reasons Stalin decided not to press the matter of Greece, the deal did not materialize because, for one thing, Roosevelt's approval, required by Stalin, was conditional and partial. We can see now that it also failed because while Czechoslovakia and Poland were not even mentioned in the agreement their fate under Stalin did not differ from that of the other countries. And what was actually left of the Western share of fifty per cent in Hungary in 1956 when the Soviet tanks crushed the Hungarian revolution? And where was the difference in degree of domination between Rumania and Hungary and Bulgaria under the massive *Gleichschaltung* to which all the countries except Yugoslavia lying within the zone of exclusive operation of the Soviet army were subjected?

(ii) Stalin's plans for Eastern Europe

By May 1945 military action in Europe had ceased; by September the Second World War had come to an end. In Europe the advance of the Soviet army had created a watertight zone, behind which it was very difficult for anyone, even the statesmen in the West, to know what was actually happening. The best example of this uneasiness and growing Western anxiety about the peculiar situation can be found in a telegram of 12 May 1945 which Churchill sent to the new President of the United States,

Harry Truman. 'Meanwhile,' he wrote in connexion with the massive withdrawal of the American forces from the Continent,

what is to happen about Russia? I have always worked for friendship with Russia, but, like you, I feel deep anxiety because of the misinterpretation of the Yalta decisions, their attitude towards Poland, their overwhelming influence in the Balkans, except Greece, the difficulties they make about Vienna, the combination of Russian power and the territories under their control or occupied, coupled with the communist technique in so many other countries, and above all their power to maintain very large armies in the field for a long time. . . . An iron curtain is drawn down upon their front. We do not know what is going on behind. There seems to be little doubt that the whole of the region east of the line Lübeck–Triest–Corfu will soon be completely in their hands.

This text is important as a description not only of the relations between the Allies and Stalin, which had deteriorated so rapidly even before the actual end of the war, but also of the situation which has since prevailed in Europe. The fateful phrase 'the iron curtain' had already been coined and by the person who should have been best informed about what was going on. If to Churchill it seemed that an iron curtain had fallen on half of Europe and if he, and the President of the United States, did not know what was happening behind it, this was a startling proof of how rapidly and how decisively the separation of the zones of operation brought into being at Teheran had produced the most feared effects.

Some authors believe that the Russians too were surprised in 1944 when the West initially ignored their request to be consulted about decisions on Western Europe and particularly on Italy, though in this case, after strong protests, they were admitted to the deliberations. Such incidents could have furnished them with further arguments in favour of keeping their own zone under exclusive control. But nothing that happened in the West resembled in any way the Russian decision taken between Teheran and Yalta to move the Polish Communist Committee from Lublin to Warsaw as an already recognized government; or the ultimatum issued by Vishinsky to King Michael of Rumania to accept a Communist Government

immediately after Yalta, in March 1945, in a Bucharest sur-
rounded by Soviet tanks.

Basically, Stalin believed that the doomed capitalist world
would, after the Second World War, enter into a phase of rapid
disintegration and dissolution amidst the collapse of the colonial
empires, the rise of the working classes and the determining
presence of Soviet Russia as the standard-bearer of world
revolution. But there were many reasons for advancing only
slowly. Stalin had to give his armies and his peoples a respite
and proceed to partial disarmament. This would also lead to a
speeding-up of disarmament and demobilization in the West
and especially to a reduction of the American forces, which was
so clamorously demanded by the American people.

American disarmament, with its corollary, the withdrawal of
the American forces from Europe, presented only advantages for
Stalin. With these prospects Stalin must have seen the wisdom
of not precipitating 'Communist revolutions' in the Eastern
European countries. For this might have resulted in a total
deterioration of relations with America and Britain, with whom
economic collaboration still presented great advantages for
Soviet reconstruction plans. It might also have frightened the
peoples of other countries, especially in Europe, where there was
a possibility that 'coalition governments', similar to those
apparently in power in Eastern Europe, might be established.
In France and Italy, for instance, the establishment of such
governments, in which key posts were held by the Communists,
could lead to a gradual Communist take-over.

In 1945 Stalin's interest in Eastern Europe was still primarily
strategic and economic. Ideological considerations were then of
minor importance, and indeed Stalin's conflicts with Tito at this
time sprang from his annoyance at Tito's 'left-wing' determination to form an exclusively Communist Government and to
proclaim Yugoslavia immediately as a Communist State. Both
these actions lessened Yugoslavia's economic contribution to
Russia, while increasing her political independence. Isaac
Deutscher described Stalin's attitude in 1945 in these words:

He was approaching the problems of the Russian zone of influence in a manner calculated to satisfy nationalist Russian demands and aspirations and to wreck the chances of communist revolution in those territories. He prepared to exact and did in fact exact heavy reparations from Hungary, Bulgaria, Rumania, Finland and Eastern Germany.*

The Soviet army was to be given priority in Eastern Europe in order to establish once and for all its new positions and lines of communication. Economic 'reparations' or 'collaboration' were to be organized in such a way as to help reconstruction in Soviet Russia. 'Mixed' Soviet companies were to be established in as many Eastern European countries as possible – Rumania, Bulgaria, Hungary, Yugoslavia – which would siphon off the resources of the respective countries directly into the Soviet economy.

Massive trade agreements with 'special' prices for the main commodities purchased by the Soviet Union, as for instance Polish coal, were to be signed under pressure. The entire region was to be put under the administrative supervision of the Soviet proconsular network: military, economic and police. Progressive denationalization and Russianization should be the aim. Finally, a type of quasi-Communist State, called a 'people's democracy' and based on a coalition of forces, controlled by the Communist parties, was to be established in the countries of Eastern Europe.

If such a relationship with the West and with Eastern Europe could be reasonably established, Stalin would not need to use the more dramatic, violent and to him more congenial means of action to which he knew he could always resort if necessary.

(iii) The units of the empire: parties and people's democracies

In Eastern Europe Stalin was soon faced not only with disorder and inefficiency in the execution of the tasks of imperial administration which he had assigned to the local Communist parties, which was only to be expected, but with a growth of

* Isaac Deutscher: *Russia After Stalin* (London, 1953), p. 79.

independence and nationalist pride which was so sudden that the situation called for drastic reconsideration.

The Eastern European Communist parties, as they emerged into the light of day after the war, differed profoundly one from the other, and, in spite of their outward discipline, were usually made up of dissenting factions. Some parties had been somewhat stifled by the repressive measures of governments before the war, while others had, on the contrary, lived in the free atmosphere of parliamentary democracy. The Bulgarian party for instance emerged as a strong cadres party, tempered in the hard school of clandestinity and illegality, intent on violence and revolution, while even before the war the Czechoslovak party was a mass party with a strong tendency towards open political organization. Some parties had been more heavily affected by Stalin's pre-war purges than others: the Polish party, for instance, suffered terrible losses in its leadership which it could not replace during the war years, and therefore during these years it was marked by a lack of self-confidence and an internal malaise; while the Rumanian party, which ever since the early thirties had been submitted to frequent changes of leadership, offered little resistance to Stalin's will and as a result emerged at the end of the war as the weakest party in Eastern Europe, with insufficient cadres and an alienated leadership.

The war also had affected the parties in different ways. The Hungarian party found that its appeals for resistance and sabotage were coldly received by the population, who in any case were far more in dread of the Russians than of the Germans; whereas the 'patriotic war' was Tito's great chance to make of the Yugoslav party the most dynamic and homogeneous of all the Eastern European parties and, by the popularity it won through the partisans, to lead it afterwards to the conquest of power.

The parties were made up inside of groups unrelated and, more often than not, hostile to each other, but in practically every one of them could be seen the same kaleidoscope. Thus in all parties one found awe-inspiring groups of Muscovites, those who had spent some of the pre-war years, but more particularly the war years, in Soviet Russia, where they had been employed by the CPSU, or by the NKDV, or by both, and whence they returned to their respective countries, maintaining mysterious links between the native party and the CPSU; then there were the natives who had, like the Rumanian Gheorghiu-Dej (who had never been to Moscow), spent either their whole life or at least the war years in their own country, either in the maquis or in prison, and who emerged soon after the 'liberation' with a strong claim to know the pulse of the party and of the country better than the 'foreigners'; there were also the characteristic groups of ex-members of the International Brigade dating from the Spanish Civil War days, who found themselves and their leaders persecuted and suspected as Trotskyists or anarchists by Stalin's secret police in Russia and in their own parties; most of them, and some other groups, had later fought in the French resistance and acquired there a quite different sense of revolutionary discipline from that which the party had expected them to show before the war and was going to ask them to show after it; and there were the few survivors of the German death camps, recognizable by their implacable violence. In many of these parties, moreover, there were exchanges and migrations of entire national or ethnic groups as a result of the territorial changes which took place at the end of the war; entire Hungarian Communist Party groups were transferred to the Rumanian Communist Party and German Communist Party groups to the Polish or Czechoslovak.

These disparities between the parties – and between the groups which formed them – crystallized rapidly around the issue of their attitude towards the Soviet Union and the CPSU, as the Eastern European Communists now faced their masters from their new position as governments of sovereign countries. Practically all the parties were divided into two main groups, not yet politically formed, but instinctively gathered together: those who wanted the party to act as the vanguard of proletarian internationalism and therefore started from the premise of active coordination with the USSR and with the other newly formed units of the European Communist dominion; and those who, on the contrary, put the specific needs

of the countries now falling under Communist rule above any
other international or ideological considerations and saw the
maintenance of the national existence of these countries as the
main safeguard against the dangers of precipitated integration.
Roughly speaking, this deep and almost subconscious line of
cleavage divided the parties into Muscovites and nativists, who
at a later stage roughly coincided with the Stalinists and national
Communists. It is known now, to take only one example, that in
the Rumanian Communist Party the Moscow group, led by Ana
Pauker, opposed the idea of the Rumanian *coup d'état* against
the Germans in 1944 and thought 'realistically' that the direct
occupation of the country by the Soviet army instead would be
a useful short cut to the Communization of Rumania, making it
unnecessary for the party to pass through the phases of 'democratic collaboration' or 'national coalition' with the other
political forces and parties in the country. This they felt would
also lead more directly and quickly towards some degree of
Communist integration with the USSR.

The rank and file – and even more so the cadres and party
machines – of the Eastern European Communist Parties were
fully aware of the enormous debt of gratitude they had con-
tracted towards the Soviet Union and the CPSU for their
installation in power. They were also fully aware of the need for
their collaboration with the USSR and the CPSU in order to
remain in power. But, in retrospect, one sees that in 1944–5 their
recollections of past relations between their countries and Russia
and between their parties and the CPSU made them apprehen-
sive of the danger of an unguarded collaboration: the danger of
being nationally and politically absorbed and annihilated. The
precedents of the Baltic States and parties were the most recent
and glaring example of what Stalin himself could do. The
Communist parties, their rank and file thought, should maintain
or create real and deep links with the peoples over which they
ruled. Above all they should show that they were determined to
ensure some national continuity and identity in their respective
countries. This was what all Communist parties and cadres were
reporting from their uneasy contacts with the already appre-

hensive peoples; and the stronger the party the stronger was the claim for the fulfilment of this demand, while the weaker the party the more apparent the need to rely primarily and solely on Soviet help and guidance.

When this diffused but unvarying information reached the more rarefied atmosphere of the leadership, it either divided the leadership itself into two antagonistic groups or, more usually, divided the minds of the leaders, who were trying to see how these tendencies could be reconciled into a single policy. This was the way in which what was to be called 'national communism' and later 'revisionism' originated: as a pressure from below, from the unanimous peoples to the rank and file and from the latter to the leadership, which in its turn transmuted it into a profound examination of how to ensure the party's stay in power by compromising to a certain extent with the population. This is also why the stronger the party the more openly was the question discussed, and the weaker the party the more stifled and repressed it became.

The issue of the form and content of the new Communist States about to take shape in Eastern Europe formed the central question, in the first years, of future relations with the Soviet Union and the CPSU. It was Tito, the first leader of a Communist party in power, and what is more a leader brought to power by his own forces, who first called the State he was about to form in 1945 a 'people's democracy'. Yet, oddly enough, and by one of these contradictions of policy which are so frequent in history, the Yugoslav party which was to be later denounced as the arch-champion of 'right-wing' policies was in a double 'leftist' opposition on this particular issue to the views of the Russians. Stalin, inspired by his policy of wait-and-see in the first years of his new collaboration with the Western Powers, did not object to the title 'people's democracy' itself. But he did not want an overt dictatorship of the Communist Party; and still less did he wish to imply that Yugoslavia had thereby become, however symbolically, another republic of the USSR. While he was pressing for the strong penetration of neighbouring Rumania and Poland and their close alignment with Soviet Russia, he was indifferent towards

Yugoslavia's claim that she was already a Communist State and as such part of the family of the Communist Republics of the USSR.

This claim concealed two assertions which hinted that Yugoslavia considered herself an equal of the mighty Soviet Union. The first protest was that Yugoslavia, as a dictatorship of the proletariat and a State with a Communist ideology, should not be treated by the Russians as an 'inferior' or 'junior' or 'politically underdeveloped' kind of State, in need of further guidance, education and supervision by the representatives of the only *really* Communist State. The second was that Tito objected directly to Stalin's recommendation that he should share, at least on paper, the exercise of power with representatives of other political forces and parties in Yugoslavia; in addition he objected indirectly to Russian intervention in what he considered to be Yugoslav affairs, in her capacity as a Great Power, who, because of her links with other Great Powers, had the right to dictate the political form and fate of a smaller country. The partisans had come to power without the Soviet army's help and had crushed the opposition of the other parties by their own dictatorship. Soviet Russia had no reason to ask them now to retreat from positions which they had won by themselves.

Tito's opposition to Stalin even on this early point gained him some popularity with the other Communist parties in the first years after the war, for he was both more to the left than the CPSU and also opposed to Russia as a Great Power. But in the end a compromise was reached and a people's democracy, even in Yugoslavia, was to be, on paper at least, a State ruled by a coalition of democratic forces.

Each of the four political forces interested in shaping the future of the Eastern European States saw in the hybrid formula of 'people's democracy' something different. Stalin, as the first and most important force, saw it as a transitional form of government during the years of collaboration with the Allies, leading to the ultimate integration of such states into the great European Communist dominion of Soviet Russia – an integration which, he thought, would require much external adjustment and many internal transformations.

Secondly, the Western Powers saw in the constitution of these States a perhaps difficult but still distinct opportunity for all the political forces of each of these countries to reassert themselves against the monolithic rule of the Communist parties; and at Yalta this is what they had demanded more firmly than before.

For the anti-Communist oppositions of the people's democracies, the pledges of the Western Powers – that within a new constitutional framework they would be reasonably free politically – were a necessary encouragement to resist the growing pressure of Communist rule. A shrewd politician, genuine democrat and Czechoslovak patriot like Eduard Beneš believed until 1947 that Czechoslovakia could continue to be a distinctively Eastern European social-democracy, unlike the Soviet State and different from the Western democracies.*

For the fourth group of forces, the Communist parties and leaders of Eastern Europe, the new people's democracies satisfied their two main criteria. They provided a system whereby the Communist parties could occupy the key positions in the State and, therefore, regardless of its title or constitution, govern it as effectively as from within an overtly Communist constitution. At the same time, the title, which was not that of a Communist republic, and also the emphasis placed on the sovereignty of the people's democracies in the basic constitutions and documents

* It is as well to observe at this point that no Eastern European Communist Government, however powerful, was able to act totally independently of the views of the older nationalist influences – the democratic parties, the Churches and the old professional organizations of farmers, workers and intellectuals. Openly, of course, the parties and the old organizations were soon to be deprived of any freedom of action; and the people themselves to be silenced by means of terror. But so enduring is the passive, even if silent, opposition of a wronged people and so obviously realistic were some of the anti-Soviet theses put forward by these national forces that they were bound to permeate the Communist parties themselves and emerge from within. What is called national communism or right-wing deviationism or revisionism is itself a proof of this, for it is only the adaptation by some Eastern European Communist parties of their Marxist–Leninist schemes to the hard facts of the situation in their countries.

did form two obvious barriers to further Soviet Russian inte-grationist moves. Here is a typical definition of such a people's democracy, given as late as 15 December 1947 by Georgi Dimitrov, the Bulgarian leader:

> Bulgaria will not be a Soviet republic; it will be a people's republic in which the leading role will be played by the overwhelming majority of the people. ... [It] will be a people's republic in which private property acquired by labour will be protected by the state authority ... but in which big capitalist profiteering private property will not be allowed to doom the labouring people to hunger and poverty. ... Bulgaria will be a ... free and independent state with its national and State sovereignty.

This independence of spirit conflicted with Russian aims on two levels. The first was administrative and economic. At the time, Stalin's main concern was that the Eastern European countries should be controlled from within by teams of Soviet administrators and experts (and from without by the regional umbrella of the Soviet army in Europe) and that they should be made to assist in Soviet Russia's economic reconstruction and recovery by heavy sacrifices, regardless of whether they were former 'enemies' or former 'allies'.

The Soviet teams were therefore engaged in these two straight-forward operations, administering and guiding the economic efforts, regardless of the national or ideological claims of the Communist parties. Indeed they behaved much more like extra-territorial outposts of imperial administration than as ideo-logical or political experts of the leading Communist State, helping other States to achieve their own Communist revolution. In the first two years the army was still the most authoritative Soviet organ in the Soviet administration of the Eastern Euro-pean empire – and the army had an even more pragmatic and direct approach, which amounted to insistence on exact and prompt delivery of goods, either as reparations or in accordance with the new bilateral trade and economic agreements signed with each of these countries. In some countries even the nationalization of industries, normally the first move to be demanded by the Communists with almost superstitious insist-ence, was opposed because of the Soviet Government's fear that it would delay the delivery of goods to Soviet Russia. At the same time pressure was exercised on the countries concerned to open their economies to the mixed companies (Soviet–Hungarian, Soviet–Bulgarian, etc.) set up by Russia in these countries. By this scheme Soviet Russia, as a shareholder, would receive the benefit of half the output of all the major branches of production of each of these countries on the basis of a neo-colonial exploitation. Finally, the systematic infiltration by the Soviet army and especially secret police agents into all the Eastern European administrations was yet another source of conflict between them and the Soviet Union.

The second level on which national attitudes conflicted with Russian authority was ideological. In so far as Soviet Russia was pressing for some more rapid revolutionary moves, and this was especially the case in Poland and in Rumania, it met with greater resistance than it expected. In Rumania this resistance was due to the obvious unpreparedness of the party, not only to proceed in the correct ideological manner, but even to install itself in power. In Poland, on the contrary, the opposition to collectivization, demanded by the CPSU experts, was founded on a firm basis of 'national differences'. In January 1947 the Polish party decided to publish a new theoretical organ called significantly *New Roads* (*Nowi Drogy*) in which the first articles were by the party's then secretary-general, Wladislaw Gomulka. The hitherto concealed conflict between the Soviet point of view and the Polish one on how to build the new society and especially on the point of collectivization now came into the open with surprising sincerity. 'We have completely rejected', wrote Gomulka, 'the collectivization of agriculture,' and he explained that this was because 'our democracy is not similar to Soviet democracy, just as our society's structure is not the same as the Soviet structure.' This bold assertion of the 'new national road' was of course to be sharply criticized by Stalin. But the fact remained that even in these first two years the stronger Eastern European Communist parties were more and more inclined to reject the Soviet example and to oppose Soviet injunctions in the light of national realities which they were quickly learning to be intractable.

Finally the Eastern European parties soon came to think of the advantages to be gained by uniting more closely among themselves and forming some kind of federal or quasi-federal bloc which, by its united strength, could defend itself better against Soviet encroachment or against the risks of a Soviet conflict with the Western world. A vague and remote idea of a neutral Eastern European bloc of Communist people's democracies could be detected in the common thinking of some of the leaders of the major Eastern European parties. This idea became increasingly precise up to 1947 when, appalled by its momentum, Soviet Russia decided to crush the heretical tendency forthwith. The episode is described at greater length in the next section.*

(iv) Stalin, imperator and pontifex

In the spring of 1948 Stalin was forced to the conclusion that things were not going well and that the problem of Eastern Europe could no longer be solved by 'persuasion' or prevarication. He had to act in three directions at once and most resolutely: in the world Communist movement, where disruption had started; in the proconsular Eastern European administration, which threatened to disintegrate; and against the renewed influence of the West, especially of the United States.

By March 1947 he must have realized that the Western world's will to resist had been aroused and that a new orientation in the policy of the Western Powers made it very unlikely that Soviet Russia could gain further positions or advantages by way of a 'power vacuum' or by the careless drifting of the Western Powers. Under President Truman, the United States had taken the historic decision to return to Europe – and for the first time in their history to commit themselves to the defence of two south-east European countries, Greece and Turkey, and of any other 'free peoples who are resisting attempted subjugation by armed minorities or by outside pressure'. This spelt a new determination on the part of the United States to re-arm and to

* See p. 30

remobilize so as to be able to cope with its new and enlarged commitments in Europe and indeed in the world. It also confirmed the American intention to help Europe to rehabilitate itself and to gather enough strength to resist the steady Soviet pressure. In June 1947, General Marshall, the Secretary of State, announced the launching of the Marshall Plan, which was 'directed not against any country or doctrine but against hunger, poverty, desperation and chaos' and which would provide economic help according to a programme which should be a 'joint one, agreed to by a number of, if not all, European nations'.

Stalin understood fully and immediately the crucial significance of these two American moves. They were a watershed in Western policy; he too would immediately have to adjust his own policies towards Europe, Western and Eastern alike, in the light of this development. This was the first step he would have to take.

His second step concerned Eastern Europe more specifically. It was directed against the disintegration of the Communist régimes there and aimed at strengthening their loyalty towards the Soviet Union. What can be called in retrospect 'the revolt of the First Secretaries' was gathering force. So many proofs of Tito's treachery towards the Soviet Union had been accumulated by the Soviet counter-espionage services and the CPSU itself that Stalin must have thought that the situation could not be redressed without the elimination of Tito and his 'clique'. In Bulgaria the veteran Dimitrov had also of late been showing signs of anti-Soviet thinking. In Rumania, Patrascanu, who could easily be diagnosed as a nationalistic, anti-Soviet plotter, was going to be crushed easily. But Gheorghiu-Dej, the First Secretary, remained for Stalin an unknown quantity, and the three other Secretaries, Ana Pauker, Luca and Georgescu, were warning Stalin against him. In Poland, Gomulka had by now come out in open defiance of the Soviet Union, and must therefore be eliminated too. In Hungary, although Rákosi was fully reliable, Rajk, who held control of the security forces, the key position in any such state, was accused by Rákosi of working for the Americans and for the Yugoslavs. In Czechoslovakia, where in any case the régime was far from being controlled from within by the Communists and where President Beneš had said as late as 6 May 1947 that Czechoslovakia was a truly democratic and Socialist State, choosing neither the Russian system nor the American liberal system, a fundamental change was obviously necessary if the country was to be held within the frontiers of the Soviet empire.

Even more serious for the Russians was the fact that some of the Communist leaders were rapidly moving towards the idea of some sort of common bond or union between their countries which could present Soviet Russia afterwards with the *fait accompli* of a Balkan or Eastern European kind of third force.

In June 1947, Tito said in public for the first time – and, significantly enough, to Western correspondents – that the 'free Balkan peoples' should form 'a strong monolithic entity'.* At the end of July Dimitrov visited Yugoslavia and on 1 August 1947 he signed several pacts, one of which made secret territorial adjustments in the region of Macedonia, the bone of contention between the two States. In November, Tito went to Bulgaria and declared that between the two countries the 'cooperation was so close that the question of federation will be a mere formality'. A fortnight later, Kostov, the then Bulgarian deputy Prime Minister, who was to be killed during the Stalinist purges in that country, said confidently that events would lead 'in the near future to the union of all south Slavs and to the creation of a common Slav country'.

In January 1949 Dimitrov went to Bucharest and on 17 January he declared there that though the time had not yet come for a federation of the countries allied to Russia, these countries would one day reach some kind of federal bond, passing first through the preliminary phases such as customs unions, etc. He cited all the countries he visualized as entering into this federative union and named Bulgaria, Albania, Rumania, Yugoslavia, Hungary, Czechoslovakia, Poland and even Greece. The reaction of some of the Rumanian Communist

* See Royal Institute of International Affairs: *Survey of International Affairs, 1947–1948* (London, 1952), p. 175.

leaders was very favourable to the scheme. (Tito had visited Bucharest only a month earlier, in December 1947.) The Polish Communist Party had also shown a genuine interest in the proposal. At the time the Poles themselves had taken the direct initiative of forming some closer links, especially economic, with Czechoslovakia, and Hungary was to join in the scheme later.

The Dimitrov interview was too much for Moscow's patience; from the Kremlin's point of view it seemed as though feverish preparations were being made for the creation of an independent South Slav – or even Eastern European – unit. On 28 January 1948 *Pravda* retorted promptly, castigating not only the idea of a federation, but also the even more modest one of a customs union. The article stated flatly that such organizations were not required and added more cryptically that what these Eastern European countries needed was to protect and maintain their independence by their own internal democratic forces. (This was a strange statement, for none of the Balkan leaders had publicly made an issue of the fact that the union between their countries would help them to strengthen and maintain their independence – against whom?) *Pravda* asked the respective countries and parties to follow instead the clear lead given by the Cominform, the newly created organ of which more will be said presently.

The third consideration which caused Stalin to act was his feeling that somehow, soon, the ideological leadership of the Soviet Union would be challenged in the Communist world at large. This was becoming obvious by 1947–8 in Eastern Europe; national leaders such as Gomulka and especially Tito were coming to the point of rejecting the Soviet dogma and proposing their own way to Socialism in defiance of the Soviet Union.

But similar threats were appearing on another horizon, in the Far East. During the autumn of 1948 Mao Tse-tung's armies had inflicted a decisive defeat on the Nationalist Chinese armies in north China and Manchuria. At the battle of Mukden in October 1948, the Nationalist armies had been decimated and the Communists won the advantage which carried them in less than a year to the achievement of total victory in the vast mainland of China: the Chinese People's Republic was proclaimed on 1 October 1949. Stalin had his first-hand accounts of the military situation and also knew of the irrevocable decision of the US Government, taken in the summer of 1948, to cut down all assistance to the corrupt and inefficient administration of Chiang Kai-shek. Stalin must have realized at once that this meant the appearance of a second Communist Power in the world – with vaster territories and a bigger population than his own gigantic Soviet Union.

Stalin's relations with the Chinese Communists had always been uneasy. As the leader of the CPSU and of the diplomacy of Soviet Russia, he had always looked on China as a strategic buffer against Japan. Twice in less than a quarter of a century he had advised the Chinese Communists to agree to collaborate with the Nationalist forces of the Kuomintang. The first time was in 1926 when the Chinese Communists were forced by the International and the CPSU to suspend their revolutionary action against the Kuomintang, with the result that Chiang Kai-shek, the leader of the Kuomintang, crushed the Communist organizations in the main towns. Mao Tse-tung with a handful of friends took command of some hundred thousand peasants and marched for more than a year until half of them, but only half, reached Yennan and made contacts with the Russians. (This became known as 'the long march' and was the birth of Mao's own party and army which was to lead him to supreme victory.) The second time was in 1945 when Stalin, for less obvious reasons, as Japan was already defeated, again advised Mao to reach an agreement with the Kuomintang. But this time Mao ignored Stalin's orders and with his own forces, like Tito in Yugoslavia and without any substantial Soviet help, began the return march, winning victory after victory.

As with Yugoslavia, Stalin knew that he had no hidden allies in the Chinese Communist Party or indeed in the Republic through whom he could direct their behaviour and ideology. The Soviet army, his indispensable lever, was not on the spot, and his secret police had no functionaries camouflaged in the

Chinese Politburo or Central Committee. It was reasonable to fear that sooner or later China would emerge as another Communist world Power and, like Yugoslavia in the West, challenge the political and ideological supremacy of the CPSU.

(v) The coercive State

In the light of these three considerations Stalin took the offensive during 1948–50 in three separate ways. First he decided to test by military means how prepared the West was to hold its main positions. This led him to the Berlin Blockade of 7 April 1948, which was defeated by the ingenious Western air-lift and by the moral resistance of the people of Berlin themselves. Afterwards Stalin ordered the Communist parties of France, Italy, West Germany and indeed all Western countries to launch a campaign of unrest against the economic stability of these countries and thereby to create pre-revolutionary situations in them. Concurrently he also denounced the Marshall Plan as an intolerable American intervention against which all European patriots should fight; and he not only refused it for Russia, but forced all the Eastern European countries, some of which had tentatively accepted it, to refuse it also.

As far as the purely political situation in Eastern Europe was concerned Stalin decided that the best way to stop the rot was to impose complete uniformity on the régimes. People's democracies, a junior variation of the Soviet State, were to be proclaimed everywhere (the last two were Rumania on 13 December 1947 and Czechoslovakia on 8 June 1948 where, respectively, King Michael and President Beneš were deposed by Soviet *coups*), and their constitutions so amended as to make it clear that they had been brought to life and remained in existence by virtue of Soviet Russia, to whom therefore they must be eternally indebted. (Even the Chinese constitution of 1948 included this formula.) Thus Dimitrov himself, whose definition of the people's democracies has already been mentioned (see p. 26), produced on 1 January 1949 a new and contrasting one:

The people's democracy and the people's democratic state ...

B

were made possible ... as a result of the historic victory of the Soviet Union in the Second World War and of the struggle of the masses under the leadership of the working class. It represents the rule of the toiling people under the leadership of the working class. [It] is a state in the transitional period, destined to ensure the development of the country along the road to socialism ... and is built in co-operation and friendship with the Soviet Union, the land of socialism.

The Eastern European people's democracies were therefore in some respects dictatorships of the proletariat, but their very existence as States and as political structures was based on the link with the Soviet Union. As dictatorships of the proletariat too their genuineness would be shown by their readiness to follow as closely as possible the model of the Soviet State and of the Soviet constitution. As *Bolshevik*, the theoretical organ of the CPSU, put it in 1959 (No. 17):

The general laws of transition from capitalism to socialism discovered by Marx and Engels and experienced by Lenin and Stalin on the basis of the record of the Bolshevik Party and of the Soviet Union are binding upon all countries.

As such the basic features of these States were: the total leadership of the local Communist party; massive and rapid industrialization; collectivization; and a coercive State.

There was no longer room in Stalin's refurbished empire for those people's democracies or Communist parties or leaders who would not accept either the commandments or the rule of allegiance and vow of gratitude to the Soviet Union. Thus, after a heated correspondence on 20 March 1948 between the Communist Party of the Soviet Union and Yugoslavia, the Cominform published on 28 June 1948 a communiqué which stated that 'the Central Committee of the CP of Yugoslavia has placed itself and the Yugoslav party outside the family of the fraternal Communist Parties' – a clear excommunication. The main accusations against Yugoslavia were: the anti-Russian attitude shown by the Yugoslav Government and party towards the representatives of the Soviet army and State in Yugoslavia; the erroneous line taken by the Yugoslav party in the essential matter of agricultural policy, where they were now refusing to collectivize and were as such becoming a 'kulak party'; and the erroneous Yugoslav view that the People's Front was an organization superior to the party itself – an error equal to that of the Russian Social-Democrats of Lenin's time.

Stalin expected that after this excommunication Tito would fall and a true Stalinist leadership would take the helm of the Yugoslav Communist Party. But Tito weathered the storm and the CPSU and Stalin were defeated. This constituted the first grave defeat of the supreme authority which Lenin and he had succeeded in imposing over the world Communist parties since the foundation of the Communist International on Russian soil and under Russian control in 1920.

Having thus so utterly failed in Yugoslavia, but in any case preferring to have the enemy outside rather than inside the empire, Stalin then proceeded ruthlessly with the purge of the 'national Communists' from all the people's democracies.

These purges, complete with self-accusations and recantations, terrified people all over the world even more than the Russian ones of the thirties had done. On 11–12 June 1948 Patrascanu was expelled from the Rumanian Workers' Party, and he was shot in 1954. On 31 August 1948, Gomulka was forced to confess his nationalistic and right-wing mistakes at a meeting of the Polish Communist Party (which he did only in part) and then was dismissed from the post of First Secretary, which was assumed by Bierut, an unimpeachable Stalinist. In November 1948 Gomulka and his friends were expelled from the party, but none was shot. In June 1949 Koce Xoxe was 'eliminated' and executed in Albania. In September 1949 Laszlo Rajk was 'eliminated' and hanged in Hungary. In December 1949 Kostov in Bulgaria first confessed his anti-Soviet crimes and his complicity with the Yugoslavs, then in a sensational *volte-face* denied his own confessions and was executed. In Czechoslovakia the purges simmered for a longer time under the surface and then started sporadically – until they reached their climax in 1950 with the 'elimination' and execution of Vladimir Clementis, the Foreign Minister, and in November 1951 of Rudolf Slanski, the former Secretary General of the party.

By 1951 the echelons of power in Soviet-dominated Eastern Europe were manned by CPSU and the NKDV agents known to be entirely reliable. In addition, the infiltration of the administrative and party machines by Soviet agents was accelerated and intensified to unprecedented degrees. At all levels and in all channels, there was direct penetration and spying by Soviet personnel.* Brzezinski describes five main categories of Soviet control:

The first link in the informal chain of imposed political control was direct consultation between the Soviet leadership and that of the countries concerned. The second was the permanent supervision of domestic events through reliance on the Soviet ambassadors. The third link was a close contact with various party organs, particularly those dealing with ideological matters, through frequent exchanges of experts and visits of Soviet 'advisers'. The fourth was the direct penetration of those governmental institutions particularly important as the instrument of power and force. And the fifth was the isolation of the various communist states from the rest of the world and from one another. All this was buttressed by Soviet military might, both in the potential and the actual sense. These controls, unlike the autonomously operative ones, were subject to purposeful Moscow direction.

Stalin's third major political act during 1949 and 1950 was the establishment of an ideological hierarchy for the entire empire. The CPSU would stand supreme in all ideological matters over all parties both inside and outside the empire. In its turn the CPSU would have only one universal source of Communist wisdom and inspiration: Stalin himself. This much was already familiar in the organization of Russia and of the International. But this time the rules were going to be applied to states and governments, creating a uniform coordinated statement of faith throughout the empire.

The first stage in the process was the founding on 22–23 September 1947 of the Communist Information Bureau, or Cominform. It contained the parties of the USSR, Yugoslavia, Poland, Czechoslovakia, Hungary, Rumania, Bulgaria, France and Italy (these last two as candidates for possible power in

* Zbigniew K. Brzezinski: *The Soviet Bloc* (New York, 1961).

their respective countries) but not the Chinese Communist Party, which had even better prospects. In January 1949 there followed Cominform's economic counterpart: the Council for Mutual Economic Assistance (COMECON).* Cominform published a journal and issued resolutions. It was through this paper and through these resolutions that the entire transformation from within of the doctrine of the 'new road to socialism' was effected. This doctrine developed into one of abject submission to and imitation of the example of the Soviet Union and the CPSU. Cominform also had the right – which was obviously useful for the CPSU – to eliminate deviationist parties. The doctrine which Cominform maintained embraced all fields of human thought and activities (as Marxism–Leninism does), from the highest and most far-fetched metaphysical questions of matter and spirit or science and human knowledge to minute prescriptions on the number of pigs to be kept on a *kolkhoz* private plot; from the etymological formation of the Slavonic languages to the use of infantry in modern warfare. Cominform ensured that, in all these matters, the Eastern European Communists as well as all Communists abroad believed not only that the CPSU knew the right and unique answers but that the CPSU itself was receiving them from one man alone: Stalin.

The abject shame of the period is now sufficiently known. Khrushchev's first secret speech at the Twentieth Congress of the CPSU – and so many more speeches on the subject – and the active de-Stalinization undertaken in countries such as Poland, Hungary or Bulgaria have disclosed much. Full anthologies of the absurd paeans of praise addressed to Stalin by all Russian, East European and other leaders of parties (including Khrushchev) are available and form one of the strangest collections of human indignity. He was called Father, he was called Sun, he was called omniscient, he was called eternal – and no adjective to be found in the literature of the mystics or of oriental despotism was thought too adulatory for this leader of an industrial state in the twentieth century. Although the technique was the same and the motives identical, never had the

* Considered in detail on p. 123.

Tsar of all the Russias been lauded in such incantations. Messianic as the Russian Orthodox might have been, never had a human being been situated on a higher pinnacle, been adored not only by his people, but by all the peoples of the world. This phenomenon has been explained by the CPSU and by Khrushchev as the form of degeneration to which absolute power can lead and has been ascribed to the progress of senility in the uncontrollable dictator himself; and this is in great part true. But some people, among them perhaps Khrushchev and his successors, may now be inclined to think that in view of the developments in Sino–Soviet relations in recent years, Stalin's course of action was perhaps also a desperate attempt to save Moscow's ideological hegemony.

2 The Revisionists (1948-57)

(i) Stalin's legacy

By 1951, the entire region of Eastern Europe in which Soviet troops were stationed was lying prostrate at Stalin's feet. Not only did no one oppose him and his rule, but all sang his praises and those of his country. In one way these were well deserved. For never before in history had Russia and a Russian ruler wielded such authority over so vast an expanse of territory. Both in the intensity with which it was exercised and in the geographical area over which it extended, Stalin's power was unsurpassed.

But how shallow was Stalin's victory in the last years of his rule ! What was described as the building of Socialism was in reality forced labour, Soviet exploitation and the production of war materials. What should have been the 'socialist transformation of agriculture' was instead the tenacious resistance of the Eastern European peasants to the expropriation of their land, accompanied by mass trials and deportations. 'Proletarian internationalism' was in fact domination and exploitation by Soviet Russia and her apparatus of quasi-occupation. And what was described as bloc coordination or even integration was the overall control by the Soviet commercial and military organizations of economies which, having just emerged from the war and its aftermath, were expected from 1950 onwards to produce again for war.

For there was war, too, though far away. In a still insufficiently explained strategic move, Stalin had, in 1950, made the mistake of allowing the North Koreans, who were Russian rather than Chinese puppets, to attack South Korea in an effort to end the partition. This partition was, in obviously smaller dimensions, a replica in the Far East of the partition of Germany in Europe. The fact that Stalin gave permission to the

North Koreans to attack is generally explained by the faulty information he received from his intelligence services to the effect that the United States, under President Truman, would not defend South Korea. Moreover, in an even more mystifying move, he instructed the Soviet delegation at the United Nations to absent itself from the meetings in which the Korean issue was discussed, thus giving to the United States and the West the enormous advantage of starting their defence of South Korea as a United Nations operation. Had Soviet Russia and her satellites been present at the meetings where this intervention was approved by the United Nations they could have easily vetoed it. Did Stalin hope to entangle the United States and Great Britain in a hopeless, slow war in Asia so as to give the Soviet forces an opportunity to strike a decisive and lightning blow in Germany and in Europe? Did he want to disperse the Western forces, exhaust their economies, unnerve their peoples and then launch the final attack? Did he take such risks because Russia, appreciably nearer the possibility of producing the atom bomb, no longer felt so inferior *vis-à-vis* the West? Or was it also a shrewder plan – more difficult to detect at the time – to allow China to become more deeply involved in a long contest with the United States and so diminish her potential demands on and rivalry with Soviet Russia?

Whatever the answer to these mysteries, the effects of the Korean war considerably aggravated the growing internal economic and even political difficulties of the Soviet bloc. It was especially in the satellites, the weakest link in the chain, that this was most noticeable. Increased demands on production led to industrial apathy, absenteeism and even strikes. The campaign for collectivization reached a painful stalemate, with the peasants entrenched in their villages. There was growing discontent and unrest among the urban populations because of the steady lowering of the standard of living and because of the lack of the basic food and consumer goods. This led to increased activity by the secret police, to successive arrests, and to deportation and internment in the mushrooming labour camps. There was increasingly outspoken contempt and hatred of the Russians and growing signs of common determination among such vast and differing groups as the workers, the students, and the intellectuals. The impact of Western propaganda increased. So did the appeal of Tito and the Yugoslavs, who were now so fully vindicated in everything they had said about Stalin's ultimate intentions and their consequences.

The signs of an impending shake-up were accumulating. Indeed, it had already begun in Czechoslovakia in 1952 with strikes and riots, which were dealt with by the local police. When the agitation spread to East Berlin and East Germany in 1953, however, Soviet tanks had to be used against the workers of this Communist State. Open revolt reappeared in 1956 in Poznan, whence it spread all over Poland and Hungary. By then, however, Stalin was dead. After a final convulsion of fear and suspicion which produced what was known as the 'doctors' purge', he had died in March 1953, one of the most timely tyrant's deaths in history. His uncertain successors, left with an undeniably difficult legacy, immediately started to dissociate themselves and their country from the crisis which they proclaimed as Stalin's personal responsibility.

The internal history of the Soviet bloc since the death of Stalin is the story of its progressive disintegration and the unchecked decline of Russian authority within it. The threat of widespread trouble, imminent at Stalin's death, has been avoided, but at the cost of a continuing series of defections. Broadly speaking these fall into three groups. Each is marked by the total or partial rejection of Russian authority by one or more Communist States, and in each case Soviet Russia has failed to bring them to heel. The first type of defection may be regarded as that of the revisionists; the second as that of the dogmatists; and the third as that of the neutralists. The latter expression, however, is coined while the phase is still crystallizing and should be accepted with some reservations.

These three movements are in many ways hostile to each other. (Indeed, Russia has recently found herself acting the role, common to decaying empires, of referee among would-be successors wrangling over the spoils.) But on the other hand the three opposing trends all have in common a firm determination not to accept under any conditions a return to the rigid authority from which they have at last escaped. Also, although each of them has had to fight its own fight in order to achieve some independence, nevertheless the later trends have benefited from the precedents set by their predecessors. They in turn are only the forerunners of future dissenters who will demand emancipation. They are also the pioneers of new ways of reorganizing the exploded monolithic authority. Finally, all dissenting and reformist movements, of whatever group, have in common the fundamental cause of their emergence. Their basic motive has been the concern of the individual leaders to save their own Communist régimes, parties and doctrines from the total collapse to which they thought the Soviet leadership was bringing the bloc. Khrushchev, as Stalin's anti-Stalinist epigone, and Tito, Gomulka, Mao, Hodha and Gheorghiu-Dej, as anti-Russian Communists, have taken this path in their respective countries to cut their losses and establish themselves more securely where they could still be in control. Each of them fought on two fronts: in the rear, where the unceasing attempts of their own people to obtain greater freedom presented the strongest threat; and in the front, where the indiscriminating, narrow-minded and egotistical Stalinist leadership aggravated all the evils and made more difficult their already difficult contacts with the people. It is this struggle on two fronts which we shall now follow in its three main phases, as they unfolded over the past decade or so of Communist history.

(ii) Khrushchev's disentanglement from Stalinism

The collective leadership which succeeded Stalin was made up initially of Malenkov, Khrushchev, Bulganin, Molotov and, for a short time in 1953, Beria. By 1955 the group was reduced to the Khrushchev–Bulganin duumvirate and by 1956 Khrushchev emerged as the sole leader. But for all these there was one overriding aim: the maintenance in power of the Communist party in Russia and in every country over which it ruled. Thus they were faced with a great task of pacification; they had to reach a *modus vivendi* with the peoples of the Soviet Union, with the Governments of the West, and with the new forces which were emerging in the Soviet bloc. To achieve this they were prepared to jettison as much of the trappings of Stalinism as might be necessary.

Khrushchev's career in particular is a fascinating study in how to demolish a crumbling top surface in order to maintain the foundations, and at the same time an equally illuminating example of how to let off steam in order to keep the lid on. So many valuable books have been written on his policies* that there is no need to restate them here except in outline, especially as the present work is mainly concerned only with his approaches to Eastern Europe.

Even while Khrushchev shared in the 'collective leadership' of 1953–6, he was shaping for himself a central position between the two more extreme tendencies: the die-hard Stalinists, and the thorough-going reformists. Between 1953 and 1955 he was one of the most zealous and convincing advocates of the reformist Malenkov's 'new course'.* But he seemed to have come to the conclusion that 'de-Stalinization' itself might become a dangerous venture if applied without discrimination.

Limits had to be defined, and on coming to power Khrushchev drew the line between the institutions of the Soviet State and society as they emerged from Stalin's rule and the methods by which Stalin had maintained the institutions in existence. Along with the fundamental institutions, Khrushchev accepted the basic elements of Stalin's overall policy. He retained collectivization but tried to make it work by ingenious if totally unspecific secondary operations such as intensive mechanization, agro-technical improvement and the extension of arable land areas. Industrialization still stressed heavy industry, but was made more acceptable to the people by higher wages, the raising of the general standard of living and a greater abundance of consumer goods. Leadership by the party remained, but was made more attractive by dissociating it from the secret police, by an increasingly genuine democratic centralism, by the rejuvenation of the cadres and especially by a greater collaboration with the intelligentsia. What he seemed to have discarded

* See Edward Crankshaw: *Khrushchev's Russia* (Penguin Special, 1959).

from Stalin's superstructure were terror, the primacy of secret police, the worship of the leader, and the aggressive and offensive attitudes of Communist diplomats. In Russia's relations with the Eastern European peoples' democracies he introduced more flexibility and diversity, but maintained the basic strategic coordination under Soviet command.

These were Khrushchev's internal problems, deriving from Stalin's legacy of the leadership of Soviet Russia. For the most part he found it sufficient in this sphere to maintain the basic principles of Stalin's policy, while attenuating his method of enforcement. But there was also Stalin's legacy of leadership of the Communist world movement. The problems here were even more entangled. The final attempt by Stalin to impose himself on the CPSU by force as the uncontested leader had brought the entire movement into a state of unrest. Besides, since the death of Stalin there were in the Communist movement now two leaders who could be considered as the 'grand old men': Mao in China and Tito in Yugoslavia. It was vital to Khrushchev that neither of these should succeed to Stalin's place on the Marxist ideological throne. Therefore, in Bulganin's company, he visited them both: Mao Tse-tung in 1954 and Tito in 1955.

The visit to China was in a sense overdue, since Stalin had never visited the new Asian Communist Power. At that time, too, in the protocol of the Soviet Union and of the CPSU China took second place in greetings and other matters of precedence. The two States were still discussing 'in a comradely way' the vast problems of their future economic collaboration, China believing or pretending to believe that Soviet Russia would even make substantial sacrifices in her own plans so as to accelerate China's development and help to bring it up to the level of Russia's own. Relations between the Russian and Chinese parties were cordial, Mao accepting by and large Stalin's main interpretations of Leninism. But even then the seeds of discord were present. Mao was adamant on the need for each Communist country to be free, within the fraternal community, to choose its own way and apply its own methods. The 'five points' which the Chinese were to present in Bandung in 1955 were all centred around sovereignty and non-interference, and they constantly brought these points forward during the Polish and Hungarian crises.

Moreover, the Chinese were implacably anti-Yugoslav. They were highly suspicious of their relations with the West and with India. They attacked as 'liquidationist' the Yugoslav abandonment of the main Leninist prerequisites: collectivization, exclusive stress on the means of production and the exclusive role of the party. To the Maoists, the maintenance of an anti-Yugoslav line was and remained the thermometer of revolutionary fervour. Thus, in later years, when the Chinese were outraged by Russia's Great Power meanness towards them over economic, technical and military assistance, they projected their differences, as usual, in ideological terms. They 'discovered' that from 1956 onwards, at the Twentieth Congress and in his secret anti-Stalin speech, Khrushchev had betrayed the cause of Communism. To them the sequence seemed clear. In June 1955 Khrushchev had visited Yugoslavia to acknowledge the failure of Russia's offensive. In the next twelve months he had denounced Stalin, dissolved the Cominform and thus started the new revisionist upheaval in Eastern Europe. Then in June 1956 he returned to Yugoslavia to renew friendly relations with her. The Maoists had good reason to think that the approval of the Chinese attitude which Khrushchev and Bulganin seemed to have shown during their visit to Pekin had been countered by the influence of Yugoslavia, the leader of Western infiltration within the Socialist camp.

Khrushchev's two visits to Yugoslavia meant two different things. The first, the State visit in 1955, was the Russian Canossa, the unmistakable proof, offered by Stalin's successors, of Stalin's defeat after seven years of unrelenting offensive against tiny Yugoslavia. It had not been merely a war of words, a matter of ineffectual trumpets blasting against the walls of an unyielding Jericho. Stalin, who never tolerated the existence of a rival, tried with all his ingenuity to destroy Tito and the Yugoslav people's democracy. He mobilized the Cominform propaganda machine for a campaign of unprecedented intensity, and launched incitements to rebellion and assassination. He did his utmost to set up and finance factions within the Yugoslav party and fostered sedition within the country. He tried to strangle it economically by imposing a complete blockade. He set up Communist Yugoslav exile organizations, giving them the use of radio stations and other means of propaganda warfare. He prepared plans for eventual military intervention. Yet, for the first and last time, he failed to chastise a rival; and the CPSU and the USSR failed to impose their authority. This is what his successors had to confess *urbi et orbi* in June 1955, startling the Eastern European world with their painful 'mission of reconciliation'.

But this was only the beginning. When he had given Tito proof of his good faith by his anti-Stalin speech at the Twentieth Congress and by the dissolution of the Cominform, Khrushchev was invited to visit Yugoslavia as head of the party and to renew relations between the two parties on 20 June 1956. This visit produced a communiqué in which the USSR openly renounced its claim to infallibility. The shock to the Eastern European bloc was profound: it opened even larger avenues of disintegration. It also alarmed the Chinese who, to counter the influence of Tito, started a campaign to reassert Russia's leadership of the CPSU in Eastern Europe.

Khrushchev's concessions to Tito paved the way for a greater disintegration, as many of his opponents had anticipated. Yet Khrushchev was not so unguarded as he might have seemed. He had a threefold plan. He set out first to consolidate, even if on a different basis, the USSR's strategic domination of the Eastern European people's democracies, Stalin's former empire (see section iii below). He then diverted some of the enthusiasm for Tito's national communism into a new, more acceptable, channel, that of a Russian-inspired revisionism (section iv). And finally he refused to acknowledge that the Russian–Yugoslav agreement to disagree was a precedent for other Eastern European parties and countries. His action in Hungary (section vi), for instance, was his most forceful demonstration of that point.

ulka when he came to power in 1956 and he reasserted
sh sovereignty in many aspects of Russo–Polish mili-
aboration. Likewise Imre Nagy, in 1956, took as his
ogan Hungarian opposition to the Warsaw Treaty.
CON was faced, at a critical moment for Khrushchev,
fierce and successful opposition of the Rumanians in
All three developments will be dealt with chronologi-
he next section of this survey.

impact of Yugoslav revisionism

visit to Yugoslavia in 1955, and in the light of all the
out the situation in Eastern Europe which he had
since Stalin's death, Khrushchev seemed to have
that the wounds inflicted by Stalin were far from heal-
were affecting directly and profoundly the immediate
of the satellites with Russia herself, and would con-
do so. It was true that by using Stalin's old precepts
ne of his methods of applying pressure, Khrushchev
enkov had secured the formation of the Warsaw Treaty
tion which entailed a new strategic hold on these
s. But this was, in a characteristically Stalinist way, an
nt obtained from the *Governments*, still made up of the
nist teams. Khrushchev must have wondered whether,
anti-Russian and liberalizing winds blowing, as they
er these countries, the Stalinist teams could remain
nger in power and whether their possibly violent fall
ot break the other links and foundations as well.
nly country in which some genuine experiments with
hods and new ideas were being made was Hungary.
divided régime had been set up in July 1953 with Nagy,
mist, as Prime Minister and Rákosi, the arch-Stalinist
-Titoist, as First Secretary. These two, with divided
although Rákosi held the whip-hand ultimately), were
rheads, and while Nagy, a genuinely idealistic Com-
was trying to bring about some improvements in the
atmosphere, in the economic situation and in the
of the Hungarian Communist Republic, Rákosi was

(iii) The strategic consolidation: the Warsaw Treaty

The treaty on 'friendship, cooperation and mutual aid' (the
Warsaw Treaty) was signed on 14 May 1955. Its signatories
were the USSR, Poland, Rumania, Hungary, Czechoslovakia,
Bulgaria, Albania and East Germany. China, although a non-
European Power, signed as an associate, while Yugoslavia, a
European country, remained outside it. Generally speaking, and
not only in Communist political interpretation, the signing of
the new treaty was attributed to Russia's concern over the inclusion of West Germany in NATO, and hence the appearance
of a coherent West European defensive organization in which
sooner or later the German Federal Republic was bound to
play a major role. Since May 1955, the European balance of
power has been measured in terms of NATO forces and Warsaw Treaty forces, and this is the most striking significance of
the agreement.

But from our point of view, the Warsaw Treaty can be more
significantly linked with another treaty signed by the USSR, on
the following day, the peace treaty with Austria of 15 May 1955.
This marked the climax of the new style of Soviet foreign policy,
the 'Geneva spirit' (although it actually preceded the Geneva
summit conference of the summer of 1955). It was Russia's
most substantial concession to the policy of 'peaceful coexistence' which she extolled so loudly. In this case (as in the case of
the evacuation of the Finnish province of Porkala) the Soviet
Union was voluntarily withdrawing its armies from a territory
which it had 'liberated' – and, moreover, it agreed to the setting
up in that country not of a 'friendly' régime, but of a neutral
one. However, the Soviet leadership was well aware of the
implications this action might have for the Eastern European
countries. Consequently it took care that, before the concessions
to Austria were made, the countries of Eastern Europe should
be bound by new commitments. These were to be found in the
Warsaw Treaty.

The new commitments were mainly contained in Article 5 of
the Treaty, which placed the armed forces of all the signatories
under a single command. A Soviet officer, Marshal Koniev, was

appointed commander-in-chief of this command as a matter of course. (He has since been replaced by another Soviet Marshal, Grechko.) Article 7 also made it very clear that the signatories were precluded from entering into any other kind of alliance. This was not only an obvious limitation of the sovereignty of the Eastern European countries, it was also confirmation of the fact that they belonged exclusively to the Soviet system and its military articulations in Europe.

Undoubtedly, the Communist Governments, especially the Polish and the Czechoslovak, had a genuine interest in organizing the mutual defence of their régimes, together with the Soviet Union, against the growing forces of Western Europe, particularly in view of the resurgence of Western Germany as a military power. But the same Governments were fully aware that the status now obtained by Austria corresponded much more to the wishes of the peoples of Eastern Europe and that to extricate their régimes from Soviet military and political control would be a very popular move for them to make.

The concept of neutrality, and even the word itself, had an electrifying effect upon the imagination of the peoples of Eastern Europe. The proof is that it became in Hungary, once freedom of expression was restored, the general rallying call and the slogan which carried Imre Nagy and the Hungarian revolution to its logical conclusion. The main Communist indictment against Nagy was precisely that he had tried to break Hungary off from the Warsaw Treaty organization, the militant Communist strategic organization in which there could be no room for 'neutrals'. Moreover, 'neutrality' was to become a forbidden expression in all these countries, and in the revised penal code of Rumania of 1958 the propagation of the idea carried the death sentence.

Thus, in May 1955, the Communist Governments of Eastern Europe had been made to redefine their positions as integral parts of the Soviet defence in Europe. In this respect, the policy of Malenkov and Khrushchev differed in no way from Stalin's. In 1955 and in the light of the reorganization of NATO, they still saw Eastern Europe as an essentially strategic auxiliary to the Soviet Union. Indeed, the Warsaw Treaty set up a Political

Consultative Committee. It was sup[...] months, and might have had the a[...] participants a better idea of the secret[...] ments between the Soviet Union and[...] committee in fact met only after two ye[...] It was not to Russia's advantage to h[...] cussed publicly, even in the supreme[...] And the joint command went as a matt[...] while all troop dispositions were to b[...] and the country concerned.

A secondary aspect of the Warsaw[...] of the presence of Soviet troops in[...] According to the peace treaties with th[...] 1947, all Soviet troops should hav[...] mediately from their territory, with[...] Soviet armed forces as Russia might '[...] of the lines of communication of th[...] Soviet zone of occupation in Austria'.[...] ing to exist, it was natural to expect tha[...] remain in the two countries. The Wars[...] new general settlement, a convenient[...] problem also. During the Hungarian re[...] the withdrawal of the Soviet troops sh[...] impatience of the Eastern Europeans t[...] use of Soviet tanks to crush the popula[...] they were to the Soviet command and[...]

Thus the Warsaw Treaty organizatio[...] by which the Eastern European States[...] Stalin's death, to the strategic policies[...] them. The other supra-national instit[...] hoped to forge all these countries i[...] pendent on direct Soviet influence, [...] streamlined Council for Mutual[...] (COMECON). Both the Warsaw T[...] gave rise to great apprehension with[...] slavia, from outside the bloc, steered c[...] Poles were equally distrustful. New[...] laboration between Poland and Sovie[...]

c

50   Th[...]

by Gom[...] full Poli[...] tary col[...] main sh[...] COME[...] with the[...] 1962-3.[...] cally in[...]

(iv) The[...]

After hi[...] facts ab[...] gathered[...] realized[...] ing and[...] relations[...] tinue to[...] and som[...] and Mal[...] organiza[...] countrie[...] agreeme[...] old Stali[...] with the[...] were, o[...] much lo[...] would n[...]

The o[...] new me[...] There a[...] the refo[...] and ant[...] powers [...] at logge[...] munist,[...] political[...] attitude[...]

bent only on Nagy's dismissal from power, which he brought about in 1955 at the cost of further exacerbating the Hungarians.

In the other countries, Stalinist teams held their own with the old methods: Gomulka, the revisionist, was still in prison; Patrascanu, the nationalist, had been shot in Rumania in April 1954; Chervenkov, the arch-Stalinist, was triumphant in Bulgaria. But the East European leaders all warned Khrushchev that if the 'new course' continued and if Tito's influence was allowed to spread, their positions would become precarious. Tito's prestige and influence were indeed rising throughout Eastern Europe. High even at the end of the war, they had risen considerably with his defiance of Stalin and with the Russian Canossa. Moreover, Tito himself was clearly going to capitalize his victory from a political point of view. He accepted the Russian visit and apology. But not only did he continue to resist Russian domination; he presented a long list of conditions for the re-establishment of more normal relations, one of them being precisely the replacement of the Stalinist leaders in Eastern Europe. Here Tito felt hopeful, for should Russia refuse to do this, his own influence might well be potent enough to bring it about. The open abandonment of collectivization in Yugoslavia as announced in 1953; the success of the workers' councils as another form of the leadership of the proletariat; the dilution of the party into a broader and more national organization – all these were of greater interest to the Eastern European Communists than Stalin's sterile and brutal methods, which Khrushchev had only attenuated. Yet it was important that Russia should give a positive lead, both for the integrity of the empire and for the ideological inspiration it could provide. It became increasingly clear to Khrushchev that some degree of liberalization in Eastern Europe was inevitable. His choice was between attempting to guide it by placing himself and Russia at its head, and trying to resist it for as long as the old guard of Stalinists could survive.

But the Eastern European problem was not Khrushchev's only one. His main concern was still with his own position in Russia: would he attain sole rule, and what would be its message and impact? As things had gone since 1953, he could on the one hand count on the support of the Russian people, of Russian youth, and of the vast and ramified intelligentsia for the main points of his positive programme. This was aimed at peaceful coexistence, liberalization within the country, and the subordination of the party *apparatchiki* to the managers, the technicians and those responsible on the spot. He knew also that, on the other hand, he commanded the party's respect for his staunch maintenance of heavy industrial production and collectivization. But still these two policies appealed to incompatible groups and could not be presented as a whole, unless some catalyst were to be found; and the dichotomy expressed itself in the deep division which was becoming increasingly visible in the leadership of the CPSU. Malenkov and his group were inclining towards further reforms, even if these entailed the risk of the party losing some essential controls and the possibility of reducing to nothing the 'Leninist' basis of the Communist State. Molotov and the diehard Stalinists were denouncing as criminal folly any attempt to introduce liberalizing experiments which weakened the Russian doctrine of the State or which allowed Tito's influence to spread in the Communist States of Eastern Europe. In fact the Russian split also mirrored the split in the Communist world outside, epitomized by the Chinese leaning decisively towards classic Stalinist doctrines and the Yugoslavs and Eastern Europeans towards new and realistic methods and reforms. Khrushchev had not yet arrived at a dynamic formulation, the right slogans and the necessary myths, which are the basic ingredients of any ideology.

It was on the eve of the Twentieth Congress, at the beginning of 1956, that Khrushchev found the way to amalgamate all these factors into a single doctrine which he hoped would put him at the head of the liberalizing forces and which he afterwards presented to the CPSU and to the world Communist movement with those dramatic and enthusiastic gestures, revelations and denunciations which will probably go down in history as his most remarkable characteristics.

He achieved this amalgamation by performing two somersaults. First he made Stalin the main scapegoat and denounced him as responsible for all the evils which had fallen upon Russia and Eastern Europe (and indeed the hatred of Stalin was much stronger in Eastern Europe than it ever was in Russia). By this means he achieved two things. He not only found a way to divert from the CPSU in general, and from Communist doctrine in particular, the blame for these failures and evils; but he also revealed himself as the arch-Leninist, so that he was afterwards in an authoritative position to defend as purely Leninist some of the basic institutions upon which Stalin had constructed Soviet society.

In a second such somersault Khrushchev was to try to take the wind out of the sails of Tito and the Eastern European national Communists' reformist spirit, and to try to hitch them to the sails of the heavy Russian vessel. Even if his policy were to acquire the label 'revisionist' in the process this would be acceptable, provided that it proved popular, workable and able to carry the day both in Russia and Eastern Europe. Dynamically applied, this policy would revive the Communist dogma and keep Russia as leader of the world Communist movement and its ideological inspiration.

One after another the first three steps were taken in this direction. The first step was the speeches made by Mikoyan at the public meetings of the Twentieth Congress in February 1956 and Khrushchev's celebrated 'secret speech'. These all denounced the 'cult of personality' and the deformations of the Communist State and society which it had produced under Stalin. But in his secret speech (which was first made public by the Yugoslavs) Khrushchev also attacked Stalin as the source of these evils and thus started the posthumous campaign against him which was later to split the entire Communist camp into two irreconcilable parts. Although Khrushchev's speeches did not contain a redefinition of relations with the people's democracies, or Russian apologies for the damage done by Stalin from this point of view, it was the condemnation of Stalin that the Eastern European national Communists waited for and regarded as the watershed. 'The Communist Party of the Soviet Union has not concentrated its efforts only upon the theoretical disclosure of the cult of personality but also upon the concrete unmasking of its supporter Stalin,' was the comment of the Yugoslav newspaper, *Borba*, of 20 March 1956, on the Twentieth Congress.

The second step intended to put Russian–Eastern European relations on a better footing was the dissolution of the Cominform. This was announced in a joint communiqué signed by all the member parties on 17 April 1956. It stated that the 'Information Bureau which they had set up in 1947 had completed its functions' and that from now on 'each party or group of parties would, in the course of developing its work in conformity with the common aims and tasks of Marxist–Leninist parties and the specific national features and conditions of their countries, find new and useful ways to establish links and contacts among themselves'. This stumbling-block was now removed from the path of future relations between the Soviet bloc and Yugoslavia, for the Cominform, after Stalin, was Tito's most painful memory.

The way was now open for the third step, the announcement of the doctrine of 'diversity' at the crucial meeting with the Yugoslavs on 20 June 1956. In 1955, Khrushchev and Tito had merely reopened relations between their two countries, but now they met as heads of parties and re-examined relations between these two parties. The 'declaration' published on that date contained the formulae which were to become the basis of the doctrines of 'diversity' in international Communism – what Gomulka had called 'the different roads', Mao 'the blossoming of a hundred flowers' and Togliatti 'polycentrism':

Believing that the path of socialist development differs in various countries and conditions, that the multiplicity of forms of socialist development tends to strengthen socialism and proceeding from the fact that any tendency to impose one's opinion on the ways and forms of socialist development is alien to both, the two parties have agreed that their cooperation shall be based on free-will and equality, friendly criticism and comradely exchange of opinion on controversial questions. With such a basis, cooperation between the YLC and the CPSU will develop primarily through comprehensive mutual acquaintance with the forms and methods of socialist construction in both countries, free and comradely exchange of experience and opinions on questions of common interest for the development of socialist practice and for the advancement of socialist thought. . . .

For outside observers such a text showed that the wheel had come full circle. The ostracized leader of the rebel 'gang' was now able to impose upon the CPSU (which had already had to undertake the unpleasant task of denouncing its own national leader and closing down its agency of control of the Eastern European parties) conditions of complete equality between the two parties and pledges of equally complete non-interference. But for closer observers, the June 1956 reconciliation between the two parties promised interesting consequences in the immediate future.

Khrushchev, and for that matter Tito as well, knew that this was only the opening of the real contest between them. Khrushchev had renounced the Stalinist claim of Russian infallibility and had in effect agreed to fight on equal terms with Tito for the ideological leadership of Eastern Europe. The prize was the possession of the ultimate influence on Eastern European – and perhaps on world – Communism. The two parties had agreed to disagree. And this decision had implications which Tito afterwards, in the wake of the crushing of the Hungarian revolution, explained very clearly: 'The declaration,' he said on 11 November 1956,

should in fact be relevant not only in our [Soviet–Yugoslav] mutual relations but also in relations with other countries. But unfortunately it has not been understood in this way. . . . In our opinion the [1956] declaration is intended for a wider circle than Yugoslavia and the Soviet Union. We warned that the tendencies which once provoked such strong resistance in Yugoslavia existed in all countries and that one day they might find expression in other countries, too, where they would be more difficult to correct.

The main question was which of the two doctrines, the Russian or the Yugoslav, would ultimately be adopted by the other Communist parties. The Yugoslavs had the advantages of popularity and doctrinal flexibility, and were credited with having a practical understanding of the small Eastern European countries which the Russians could never acquire. But their potential friends had been decimated in these countries, and those who had survived were still either in prison or kept on the outskirts of the spheres of influence by the entrenched and possibly Russian-inspired old Stalinist teams. Tito expected to find proof of Khrushchev's sincerity in the near future in his dealings with such personnel in the people's democracies. Disappointed in this and realizing that he was riding an insecure wave of popularity, which ebbed abruptly after the Hungarian revolution, Tito was determined to extend the influence of his doctrine especially over the neighbouring countries and parties. The Yugoslavs' position was strengthened by the fact that they had won the status of full equality for Yugoslavia and had remained outside the two 'coordinating' Communist organizations in Eastern Europe: the Warsaw Treaty and the Council for Mutual Economic Assistance.

Khrushchev in his turn seems to have been fully aware that both he himself and the CPSU had reached a cross-roads. Now he had openly changed direction and had set his party on an entirely new tack. He no longer insisted that the CPSU was infallible and had never erred; on the contrary, he had criticized and denounced the man who had led it for more than thirty years.

Looking back, this was indeed a formidable change to make. Within Russia, his criticism of Stalin was a popular move. But when that criticism reverberated abroad it was explicitly and implicitly taken to be criticism of the USSR *per se*. This was unpalatable not only to Molotov and the die-hard Stalinists, but to all the Russian and party officials or emissaries abroad. For a while Russian approaches to the changes to be brought about in Eastern Europe were contradictory to the point of incoherence. While they were promising both at home and abroad diversity and freedom of choice, the Russians were still pressing the Eastern European parties to carry on with, for example, collectivization and advising them to keep their doctrine free from any taint of Yugoslav revisionism. While at home they were eliminating from their ranks the Stalinists entrenched in positions of responsibility in the party, administration, and especially the secret police, they were doing nothing decisive to eliminate from the posts of leadership in the people's democracies persons appointed by Stalin and still governing in Stalin's best tradition. However, Khrushchev believed that, by injecting the slogans and attitudes of Eastern Europe into Russian Communist doctrine, he could place Russia once more in an ideological lead that would stand comparison with its lead in military power, industrial advance and technical know-how. Moreover, he believed that strategically and politically Eastern Europe was a zone which Russia could not afford to lose. And from another point of view, he saw it as a grouping of peoples with whom Russia had more in common and with whom she could communicate more easily than with the massive and impenetrable Chinese. Hence he allowed greater flexibility in Russia's relations with these countries. He needed, however, more time to find the new people who, while faithful to Russia, would also be prepared to show abroad the flexibility which he himself was trying to apply in Russia. But as events were to show, time was very short and the number of suitable new, more sophisticated, leaders of the Eastern European parties was small, if he were not prepared immediately to recognize the 'Titoist' wing.

Russian–Yugoslav relations were watched particularly by the Eastern European leaders. Leaders and cadres who had survived the Stalinist purges of the forties could hardly believe their ears when they heard the new language of Communism. At the same time the peoples of Eastern Europe, stimulated by the undeniable Russian concessions, if not capitulations, were bringing from within and from without increasingly stronger pressure to bear in order to obtain minimal economic and political reforms and to redress the evils perpetrated by Stalin and his Russian agents. The situation in Poland and Hungary had been steadily mounting towards a climax and indeed less than ten days after the publication of the Belgrade communiqué riots started in Poznan.

Finally, according to the revelations made in the recent

polemics with the CPSU, the Chinese Communists have shown that they detected, even at the time of the secret speech, that Khrushchev, behind his de-Stalinization campaign and in spite of his maintenance of the socio-economic basis of the dictatorship of the proletariat, had embarked on a doubly dangerous path. He was obviously allowing revisionist tendencies to penetrate the Marxist–Leninist doctrine, a fact which would lead sooner or later to its disintegration. He was also giving greater consideration and help to the Communist States of Eastern Europe than to China's own industrial and economic development. The Chinese were prepared to watch these ominous features and in the course of the next two years, 1956–7, they supported Khrushchev from time to time, hoping that he would return, with their help and guidance, to sound Leninist–Stalinist principles. But by 1958 they realized that the wrong turning he had taken in 1956 was irreversible and as far as they were concerned was leading rapidly towards the doom of Communism.

(v) Poland: revisionism by revolution

The pressure of the Polish people against its rulers and against Russian domination had mounted steadily in Stalin's last three years. But it gained a fresh impetus after de-Stalinization began in Soviet Russia, and eventually burst out in the Poznan riots of 28 June 1956. These in turn forced a dramatic political reorientation between 18 and 28 July and culminated in the crucial meeting on 19 October between Gomulka and Khrushchev, at which Khrushchev accepted Gomulka's revisionist régime. For Poland this marked the hopeful beginning of its national emancipation: 'Spring in October' as it was then called. For Khrushchev, even if he did not approve initially of everything that the Polish Communists were doing, it marked the beginning of Soviet-approved and Soviet-controlled revisionism in at least one East European country.

Economic discontent, the liberalizing example of Russia's 'new course' and the inspiration of the Polish intelligentsia had all brought pressure to bear on a weak and divided Government, which had been headed during the Stalinist years by the unanimously disliked Berman and his group of staunch pro-Russian Stalinists.

The initial discontent arose from a steady deterioration of socio-economic conditions. This was a prime cause of the Poznan workers' riots, but it became much more vocal as a result of the official attitude at the subsequent trials. Neither Polish nor Russian Communists, at the trials or subsequently, attacked the workers' arguments as 'counter-revolutionary propaganda' or 'Western-imperialist instigated', for both were acutely conscious of the economic shortages underlying the rising. Moreover, the Polish Communists were beginning to argue that there was very little that they could do unless and until the Russian ideologists allowed them to change from within the entire pattern of economic life in Poland, starting with the abandonment of collectivization and ending with the re-orientation of the industrial plans towards the production of consumer goods; and to change fundamentally the terms of their economic collaboration and trade with Soviet Russia, which was one of the main causes of the stifling of economic life.

The second development which encouraged opposition to the régime was, ironically, the very exhortations of the Malenkov–Khrushchev leadership itself, which was directly urging the old Stalinist teams in Eastern Europe to follow their example in opening new relations with the 'working classes' by creating better economic conditions, a higher standard of living and a more genuine sense of freedom and of participation in the communal life. But Khrushchev himself would have been embarrassed if asked exactly how far such measures could go without running the risk of endangering the foundations of Communist rule. Nor could he say which Communist personalities would be able to win the trust of the people but still be fully loyal to the Russians.

In addition to encouraging resistance to their leaders among the Polish people, the Russian 'new course' similarly affected the Polish leaders themselves. It produced in them a stronger desire for national autonomy, a sense of grievance against the Russians and a sense of embarrassment in front of their own people. They were surprised and almost relieved to discover that Stalin had been declared mistaken. But none the less they envied a party which had sufficient autonomy to criticize itself in public and to reopen the 'dialogue with the people'. The fact that the Polish party was not in a position to do this was seen by the Poles as a proof that it was only a subsidiary organization, lacking the power of decision and the freedom of action which the Russian, Yugoslav or Chinese parties, all free from foreign control, enjoyed.

They thought that their feeling of inferiority was justified by the findings of a special committee set up to investigate the conditions in which the Communist Party of Poland was dissolved in 1938. These were made public at the Twentieth Congress of the CPSU in February 1956. The report stated that the accusations against the liquidated leadership were 'based on material which was falsified by subsequently exposed agents' and that 'the party honour of the comrades had been reestablished and that they had been fully rehabilitated'. It was thus recognized that the Russians, secret police or party, had disposed of the entire Polish party and liquidated and remade it according to their own wishes and interests. This was paralleled by a series of earlier revelations made by an official of the Polish security forces, Colonel Swiatlo, who defected to the West and gave a full description in 1954 of the real state of affairs. This demonstrated that the ignominious subordination of the 1930s was still evident in the 1950s. He showed that the security forces in Poland, which in the Stalinist years had more power than the party itself, had been entirely subordinated to and controlled by the Russian security forces. The truth of these revelations, broadcast to Poland by American radio stations, was subsequently confirmed by the embarrassed speed with which the Ministry of Public Security was abolished in Russia and replaced, after Beria's fall, by a more normal Ministry of the Interior. Finally, Khrushchev's visit to Yugoslavia in 1955 and the declaration of June 1956 (see page 54) made their full impact on the Polish nation, including the Communists, who began to wonder why their own party could not attain the level of dignity of the Yugoslavs. All looked once more to Gomulka, who in

1947 had gone very far in advocating an exclusively 'Polish way'.

The main effect of the 'new course' was to inspire ever-widening criticism of the régime by intellectuals, and this ultimately sparked off the open resistance of the workers themselves.* The intellectuals who took the lead were mostly Communists and thus of course constituted a privileged category (the poet who made the greatest impact, Adam Wazyk, had been a conformist Stalinist until in 1955 he underwent his own personal Damascus). This is why the discussion was, as it were, largely confined to the question of what a genuinely Polish Communist régime should be and did not extend openly to the question of whether a Communist régime was in itself suitable at all for Poland. But ideas have a life of their own and meanings valid for all points of view, and, self-circumscribed as the debate may have been, what was really being discussed was the immediate need for freedom in Poland and the possibility of achieving this.

Two categories of intellectuals were the most active: the artists, writers and philosophers; and the economists.

No one who writes the history of Communism in Eastern Europe can do so without paying homage to the behaviour of the Polish and Hungarian 'creative intelligentsia'. No other Eastern European cultures have absolved themselves from the indignities of dictatorship and censorship with such an explosion of collective talent and vehement artistic dissent. The part played by the Polish literary circles and by the periodicals in starting 'the revolution' remains an example for everyone. It showed that not only in mass cultures such as those in which we all live today, but even in totalitarian cultures, the initial contact between a few men courageous enough to open their minds and discuss their problems even in a small company creates an unexpected and ever-increasing response and achieves widespread results which no sponsored initiative can ever achieve. Perhaps it is not so much the individual members or their words as the Polish Crooked Circle and the Hungarian Petöfi Club

* In Hungary, where similar developments were occurring, the same process could be seen (see page 68).

which will go down in history as part of the European fight for freedom. The ideas debated in their crowded rooms ranged over the entire field of social problems.

The ideas of the economists were among the boldest and the most fruitful. Their unanimous verdict against collectivization was understood both by the farmers and the Communist parties, and in the autumn of 1956 collective farms were disbanded in both Hungary and Poland. Their discussions on how to ensure the participation of workers in industrial management without using political controls and without the intervention of the State or the party as compulsory intermediaries were understood by the workers as an encouragement to set up Workers' Councils. (In both Hungary and Poland in the autumn of 1956 Workers' Councils flourished spontaneously.)

The part played by the industrial workers* in the Polish revolution was crucial. They were the most massive, influential and dynamic element of the Polish people's democracy and, as in East Germany in 1953 and in Hungary in 1956, once they moved the whole country moved. Roused by shortages, low wages and exploitation by the State-employer, on and after 28 June 1956 the Poznan workers rioted openly against the Government, behind banners proclaiming the slogan 'bread and freedom'. Their decisiveness and boldness prevented the régime from taking measures which might have crippled the revolutionary action, for as in East Berlin and Budapest the national police force and the armies refused to fire on the workers. The régime was faced with the choice between remoulding itself according to popular pressure, and calling in Russian troops.

The situation in Poland after Poznan was rapidly becoming revolutionary. All classes were on the move. The forces of State repression were becoming less and less reliable. In addition the political personnel was of low calibre. The two leaders to whom

---

* As usual the workers in the towns were much better equipped than the farmers and peasants to react to the political crisis and to organize themselves as an active force in the fast-moving developments. The rural population followed only later.

the various strata of society could have looked for guidance and advice were both unavailable. The Primate, Cardinal Vishinsky, was still in confinement and the Communist Gomulka was free but out of reach. The Communists, both Russian and Polish, who recognized the signs of a revolution saw the writing on the wall.

A rapid succession of events led to the *dénouement*. Between 18 and 28 July, the Seventh Plenum of the Central Committee took place and Gomulka was invited to take part. This was probably the most wide-ranging and hard-hitting debate in the history of any people's democracy, as it turned again and again around the question of how to evade two terrible alternatives which faced the party, complete anti-Communist revolution, or Soviet intervention, by finding some way of appeasing the people. On 20 July Bulganin and Zhukov appeared, in the guise of an official Soviet delegation to commemorate Poland's liberation. Bulganin's approach was the usual Soviet one on such occasions: 'Every country can go a different way to socialism,' Bulganin thought fit to say in his message, 'but Soviet Russia cannot permit this to be used to break up the solidarity of the peace camp.' The deep changes which had already taken place in Polish public opinion without the knowledge of the Russians can best be assessed by the outraged reaction that this statement – which would have been considered routine Soviet rudeness only a few months before – provoked in the country. At the same time, Bulganin offered, again in a routine Soviet way, a Russian gift of consumer goods worth some ten million pounds so as to improve economic conditions. This was both too late and too little. What remained from Bulganin's visit was the revulsion which it created in Poland at large and the determination it helped to create in the leadership of the Polish party. This was still holding its plenary meeting and, divided as it probably was between Stalinists and revisionists, it none the less became convinced that something radical had to be done to halt both the growing unrest of the Poles and the protracted callousness of the Russians. A resolution was issued on 28 July which vaguely pledged the party to bring about more liberalization and to reduce the bureaucratic control of the party, but it contained scarcely any precise answers to what Gomulka later described as the two main questions under consideration: '(1) the problem of Poland's sovereignty and (2) the problem of democratization within the framework of the socialist system.' Neither did the Seventh Plenum clarify the third question in everyone's mind: what of Gomulka's own position and future?

Soon afterwards, Ochab, the former Stalinist-appointed First Secretary, left for Yalta; from there he went on to Pekin. It is known now that in this interval the Chinese Communist Party, although in principle opposed to the revisionist tendencies of the new Polish leadership, did encourage it to make a stand and to assert a new national policy. The Chinese, according to what is now regarded as reliable information, advised the Russians during the crisis to accept Gomulka's leadership and policies and not to use force to bring Poland to heel.

The encouragement and backing the Chinese gave to the Poles also fitted in with their general attitude of helping, within the Communist bloc, any independent party which offered sufficient guarantee of maintaining the, to them, essential 'Leninist principles'. On his return from Pekin, in view of the rapid changes which were taking place in both Poland and Hungary, Ochab came to the conclusion not only that Gomulka's policies were the right ones but that they should be applied as soon as possible and by Gomulka himself. On 13 October, a meeting of the Politburo was held, with Gomulka present, and it was agreed that another Politburo be formed, including Gomulka and excluding Rokosovsky. This latter decision alarmed the Stalinists, who informed the Soviet Ambassador. He invited the Polish leaders to go to Moscow, an invitation which they declined. A *coup* organized by the Stalinists for the night of 18 October was foiled by the direct intervention of the Warsaw workers and especially those of the car factory Zeran. These intercepted the orders to arrest 700 'plotters', warned all of them, helped them to hide, and then sent emissaries throughout Poland to inform the country of what was happening in Warsaw.

On 19 October a Soviet delegation formed by Khrushchev,

Kaganovitch, Mikoyan and Molotov landed, unannounced, in Warsaw. Simultaneously Soviet troops and tanks started moving towards the capital. We now know that at the meeting between the Poles and the Russians Khrushchev accused Ochab of treachery because he had not informed him of the extent of the deterioration of the situation in the country and of the changes which had been made in the leadership of the party. Ochab replied that in Poland the reforms intended to set the country on a truly anti-Stalinist line must of necessity be more rapid and more radical that in the USSR. Then it was left to Gomulka to explain the new 'revisionist' policy for Poland which the Central Committee was about to proclaim and to convince Khrushchev that not only was it far from undermining the basic Soviet–Polish collaboration but that it was probably the only way to enable Poland to remain a Communist country in the Communist bloc. His explanations were accepted. The Soviet delegation left and the Soviet troops returned to their bases on 20 October. A formal communiqué was issued, noting the general agreement but mentioning that soon further talks would be held in Moscow (which were eventually postponed because of the far more menacing situation in Hungary).

Gomulka was elected to the Politburo and appointed General Secretary. On 21 October he presented his main political and economic programme. It brought to Communist Poland more flexibility and moderation in relations between the ruling party and the farmers, workers, intellectuals and the Church than any other Communist country could claim. It gave a new impetus to original thinking in Communist parties and countries. For at least five years it put Poland ahead of all the other countries in the Soviet bloc in matters of national independence and ideological initiative. The Polish Communist Party maintained itself in power with obvious difficulty but avoided the drama of the Hungarian revolution. It has since defended the basically non-Communist reforms adopted in 1956 against Soviet pressure. In other words the Polish party was and remains a steady example of Communist revisionism at work.

Why did Khrushchev accept this programme on 19 October?

To a great extent he had no choice. To this must be added the fact that, having already accepted, at some cost, the Yugoslav precedent of a non-Soviet type of Communist State, there was no reason why he should not accept a second one. Moreover, had he decided on intervention, he would have had, apart from some serious international complications, major difficulties with Tito, to whom he had just promised that he would respect 'the different ways to socialism', and with Mao too. And, as was to be shown so soon in Hungary, what mattered was that the Communist party should remain in power. Here Gomulka gave a promise and kept it. It was even more important that Gomulka and the Polish Communist régime should refrain from challenging the main strategic and diplomatic bonds between the two countries. Finally, Khrushchev may have begun to see himself more and more as the leader of a progressive 'commonwealth' of nonconformist Leninist States, outstripping Tito in this position and leaving Mao well behind in his dogmatic superstitions.

Why on the other hand did Gomulka agree to stop half-way towards complete Tito-like emancipation of Communist Poland from Soviet tutelage? There were three main reasons. In his conception Poland's geo-political position was such that it must lean on a genuine alliance with the Soviet Union in order to be able to protect itself against another German attack or, as has occurred so many times in Poland's history, partition between Russia and Germany. The second reason was that he wanted to avoid another Soviet occupation, and he was fully confirmed in his fear of this by Russia's behaviour in Hungary immediately afterwards. The third was that he saw with great clarity, as a Communist, that only his revisionist policy would be able to maintain the Communist party in power.

Why did the Polish people, the real force of revolution which had imposed these changes on both the Russians and the Polish Communist Party, stop short and not try to advance beyond Gomulka's self-defined limits and achieve a final emancipation from both servitudes, Russian and Communist? For two reasons, the second of which is in part a corollary of the first. The first lay in Poland's geo-political position. Soviet intervention was the most obvious countermove to any attempt at total emancipation. Soviet intervention would have been the outcome of Khrushchev's visit of 18 October, had not Gomulka convinced him that the essential links between the two countries would be maintained. What could the Poles oppose to the whole might of the Soviet army? What had Poland opposed in her long and martyred history to the repeated Russian interventions and occupations, apart from the legions, renewed with each generation, of Polish youth, killed, deported or imprisoned by the Russians? Of course, if the West could have pledged itself to help the Poles and had warned Khrushchev that it would consider Russian intervention to be a *casus belli*, the proposition would have been entirely different. But the West, which had been launched into the Second World War because of its pledge to Poland, could not conceivably be swept into a third one for the same reason and in such very different conditions. It seems evident that such friendly advice as Poland may have received from the West at the time amounted only to a call for patience and hope for gradual improvement. Likewise the Catholic Church, a body with enormous influence, increased by the political vacuum created by the Communists, advised the Poles through Cardinal Vishinsky to show moderation. It has been said that the political equation of Poland was based on two factors: the Cardinal and the Commissar, Vishinsky and Gomulka. The fact is that in the circumstances of 1956 these two leaders of opposing movements, both actually emerging from the confinement in which they had been kept by Stalin's agents, found a common denominator in their sense of responsibility towards their compatriots. Moreover, the Soviet intervention in Hungary soon became a further reason in itself for the Polish patriots not to exert more pressure and on the contrary to try to consolidate the position they had won.

The second reason why the people did not press the revolution farther is that the Polish Workers' Party (and its ramifications in the army and security forces, the trade unions and the intelligentsia) was, in 1956, the only organized political force in the whole of Poland. It could, and did, channel the mounting opposition. Also, acting in concert with the diffuse mass of patriots, it imposed from within upon the Russians and the Stalinists several immediate and far-reaching reforms. These included freedom for the peasants, freedom for the Church and freedom for the intellectuals; and it pledged itself to grant later more freedom for Parliament, considerable economic improvements, intensification of relations between Poland and the West, and, above all, the steady continuation of the liberalization at home. But the condition was that it should be Gomulka, the party leader, who was to be trusted to do this.

The fact remains that if the party and Gomulka had switched their support to the Stalinists and the Russians, the events which took place between July and November 1956 would have been entirely different and their results, in all probability, worse rather than better.

(vi) Hungary: revisionism by intervention

In the Polish crisis it is not entirely clear how much of the final settlement was achieved by compromise between the frightened Khrushchev and the indomitable Poles. In the Hungarian crisis, which followed closely, it is clear that Hungary would have been entirely lost to the Soviet empire had Soviet Russia not used the direct means of military intervention as a Great Power in a zone of domination.

The opposition of the Hungarians to the idea of being governed by a Russian-guided Communist administration sprang from deep-seated roots. Like the Rumanians and East Germans, and unlike the Poles, Bulgarians, Yugoslavs and Czechoslovaks, the Hungarians have no common Slavonic link with Russia in their history. As a result the sufferings of the Hungarians under the Russian occupation were that much worse than those of their neighbours. Also they were aggravated by the long military action on Hungarian soil beforehand and by the subsequent loss of that part of Transylvania which had been ceded to Hungary by Hitler and Mussolini in 1940. (One of the reasons for the popularity of the Communists in Hungary after the First World War was their policy of 'self-determination up to secession' which came so near to Hungarian irredentism.)

Like the Czechs, the Hungarians had an open frontier with the West, made longer by the Austrian peace treaty in 1955; and this, immaterial as it might ultimately be in terms of strategy and *Realpolitik*, was a stimulating thought for a people in search of freedom. Moreover, for the Hungarians, who had fought two world wars on Germany's side, the reappearance of West Germany in full economic stability, political influence and military importance in Western Europe was a stimulus, while for the Czechs and the Poles a revived Germany was an instinctive cause of anxiety. Like Germany, the Hungarians considered that all the evils of their situation arose from the Versailles Treaty, which had been for the Poles, Czechs, Yugoslavs, and Rumanians their birth certificate in contemporary Europe. All these factors meant that when, after Stalin's death, events took a different and more rapid turn, Hungary was to be the country in which, from the beginning in 1953 and until the end of the phase in 1956, these events were going to take the most dramatic form.

To keep this brief reconstruction of the Hungarian crisis as simple as possible the period concerned is here divided into four phases. The first phase, running from July 1953 to April 1955, covers the first premiership of Imre Nagy. The second phase, from April 1955 to July 1956, covers Rákosi's last period in office. Rákosi was dismissed for good in July 1956. Then started the third period, from July 1956 to 30 October 1956, during which Gerö and Kádár took the leadership of the party, while Nagy was only slowly brought back into it and finally on 24 October made Prime Minister. In the fourth and last phase, which lasted only from 30 October to 5 November 1956, the fateful week in European history when Britain and France tried to intervene in Suez and Soviet Russia intervened in Hungary, the anti-Communist revolution was crushed.

(a) *The first premiership of Nagy*

Imre Nagy, who was a Communist of long standing, a friend of the arch-Stalinist Rákosi, and himself regarded as a Stalinist, was in many respects a typical Central European intellectual who liked nothing better than long discussions on theoretical problems. He emerged during the general collapse produced by the harsh Stalinist policies of 1949–53 as one of the spokesmen for the minority in the Secretariat of the Hungarian Communist Party opposed to Rákosi's excesses. He drew his inspiration from his own observations and from the reports made to him by his non-Communist friends, and he moved slowly towards a doctrinal or political crystallization, which occurred only in 1953 under the influence of the Malenkov–Khrushchev de-Stalinization in Russia.

(Indeed the parallel between Nagy's career and Malenkov's is a close one throughout. Like Malenkov, Nagy was one of those individuals so divided within himself that he could lead tyrants, like Stalin and Rákosi, whom he deeply despised and whose policies and methods he later abjured, to believe that he was a faithful lieutenant. Like Malenkov, Nagy too was soon swept away by the emotional and logical consequences of the initial criticisms and adjustments proposed within the 'Leninist' framework, and was eager to go beyond them – to modifications which to a 'Leninist' would be anathema, but which to any objective observer would merely confirm that 'Leninism' itself is based on insoluble contradictions. Finally, like Malenkov, he had a hesitant cast of mind and seemed to be not always in good health. Twice Rákosi outmanoeuvred him when he was ill and unable to attend crucial meetings.

Nagy was brought to power during Malenkov's premiership, and based his policy and thinking upon Malenkov's 'new course', for which he thought he could produce a Hungarian variation. Likewise he fell from power in 1955 when Khrushchev reasserted a more 'Leninist' policy over Malenkov's one of drift. This enabled Rákosi to get rid of him and to set him on his final voyage to disaster. This circumstance is significant in itself. But it is also important to observe that at the beginning of the irreconcilable split between the two wings of the Hungarian party, both had their correspondents and patrons in Moscow. Their actions reflected, if they were not the result of, the triangular fight within the Soviet leadership: the no-change policy of Molotov and his followers; the costly 'new course', of Malenkov; and Khrushchev's conditional de-Stalinization.)

Nagy's initial programme in 1953 resembled Malenkov's new course in stressing the need for economic improvements and the relaxation of the party's controls and demands. He pursued a relaxation of the policy towards the farmers (Nagy himself was an agricultural expert); and he sought a 'consolidation of legality' towards the citizens, by curbing the secret police, closing down the labour camps and gradually emptying the prisons in successive amnesties. This programme at once fired the enthusiasm of the Hungarian workers, youth and intelligentsia. Much to Rákosi's displeasure, it gave rise to an extraordinary ferment in all the clubs and journals which discussed the subjects. They enlarged their scope to include the painful problems of how far democracy could progress in a Communist State and how far a people's democracy could reach sovereignty within the Soviet bloc. This approach, undertaken regardless of Russian reactions (Nagy was appointed premier after a pessimistic report made by Rákosi to Malenkov, Khrushchev, and the Soviet leadership in Moscow in June 1953), brought Hungary to the forefront of the countries and peoples of Stalin's empire. The Hungarian debate preceded the Polish one by a good year or so, and although the influence of the two series of events on each other is so intricate that it cannot be completely disentangled it seems fair to say that until Nagy's first fall from power, in 1955, it was Poland which looked to Hungary for example and guidance. By then, under the double pressure, of their own people from within and of the Russian 'new course' from without, East Germany, Rumania, Bulgaria and Czechoslovakia had taken some measures towards a kind of liberalization, though, generally speaking, they weathered the entire stormy period of the 'new course' as 'loyal satellites'.

During the two years of Nagy's first Government, Rákosi never laid down his arms. He was deeply stung by jealousy and also convinced in his primitive mind that such tightrope exercises could only lead to the total fall of a régime exclusively, though precariously, founded on terror. Hence he did his best from within to sabotage the reforms which Nagy wanted to initiate. He was in control of the party and proceeded with new gusto to strengthen its apparatus while similarly reinforcing the secret police and the army, which he controlled through the detested General Farkas. This produced more and deeper lines of cleavage in the already disintegrating Communist body politic. It exacerbated the hostility within the party between Rákosi's majority and Nagy's minority. It forced the latter to rely more on the State administration, which began to think of itself as a rival organization to the party. It made the repressive forces – security police, army, etc. – even more mistrustful of the population. Above all, it cut off the entire Communist body politic from the nation. While Nagy wanted more power, Rákosi was trying to weld the dwindling and shrinking forces of the Communist rule into a striking force of terror.

(b) *Rákosi's last tenure of office*

In the spring of 1955, Khrushchev's stand against Malenkov's hesitant new course in favour of the maintenance of the Leninist fundamentals of heavy industrialization, collectivization and leadership of the party (explained to the other Communist parties in a document circulated by Khrushchev), together with Malenkov's disappearance as a personal influence in Nagy's favour, convinced Rákosi that the moment had come to recapture the lost positions. He dismissed Nagy – absent through illness – by means of the usual Communist palace intrigues, and took both levers of command into his own hands again.

Nagy, who was undergoing his second change of ideological orientation, from the new course to a genuine national Communism, did not resist the manoeuvre to any extent. On the contrary, he started to write a report to the Central Committee on his new views and opinions (this was afterwards published as a book *On Communism*). The salient point of this work was its handling of the problem of sovereignty in a Communist country. Even at this time, Nagy went so far as to see Hungary, as he saw Yugoslavia, acting as an independent and neutral country on the basis of 'an active co-existence of progressive democratic socialist – or similar – countries with those other countries having a different system. This was to be achieved through a coordinated foreign policy and through cooperation against the policies of power groups'. He may also have shrewdly calculated that, in any case, in spite of Malenkov's defeat at Khrushchev's hands, Rákosi's Stalinist methods were doomed. They were doomed in Hungary because the revolt of the intellectuals had now gained such proportions, through the Petöfi circles and through the sharpening of ideas and polemics, that the flagging party could no longer contain and stifle it. Moreover, they were doomed in the Communist bloc at large, as the rapid anti-Stalinist movement began to gather decisive momentum. Then came the Twentieth Congress (which re-habilitated Béla Kun, the Hungarian leader purged by Stalin in the thirties and a former enemy of Rákosi), the secret speech against Stalin, the dissolution of the Cominform (in which Rákosi had been operative) and the reconciliation – or what amounted to this – between the CPSU and the Yugoslav League (who considered Rákosi as one of those most responsible for their persecution). Finally came the rapid and breath-taking developments in Poland. Nagy had good reason to believe that events would soon require him again.

It was at this juncture that the Hungarian problem began to appear as a triangular contest between the Russian Communists, the Yugoslav Communists and the Hungarian revolutionaries, each desiring to mould Hungary according to their own ideas. This brings out a basic difference between the Hungarian and the Polish crises: the latter had been a straight contest between the Poles and the Russians, Gomulka being strong enough to find his inspiration in the Polish reservoir of ideas and Tito having for Gomulka enough respect and trust to be content merely with his ultimate success. But in Hungary, Tito had a direct interest in removing Rákosi, one of his arch-enemies; and, unlike Poland, Hungary was Yugoslavia's neighbour. Tito showed his interest very clearly. 'When we were in Moscow,' he said on 11 November 1956, 'we said that Rákosi's régime and Rákosi himself had no qualifications whatever to lead the Hungarian State and to bring about inner unity, but that, on the contrary, their actions could only bring about grave conse-quences. Unfortunately the Soviet comrades did not believe us.' He insisted that a change of personnel be effected in the leader-ship of the Communist Party and Government in Hungary, without which relations between the Hungarians and his own party and country could not be improved. Moreover, a declaration by the foreign policy editor of *Tanjug* on Hungarian developments on 4 November 1956, which was also the first official Yugoslav statement to appear after the crushing of the Hungarian revolution by the Soviet tanks, said that 'our interest results from the fact that our country is a neighbour of Hungary and that our people are not indifferent to how events in that neighbouring country will develop, a country with whom we have had experience of a negative and positive kind in the past.' Those who were to be in charge of the new Hungarian policy should therefore be approved by Tito, and their policies should be akin to those of Yugoslavia. Although there was no longer open hostility between the CPSU and the YCL, their policies still differed substantially in some respects: the Yugoslavs wanted to decollectivize; to replace the party by a broader national organization; and to develop the workers' councils into a kind of alternative to the party-controlled 'dictatorship of the proletariat' as a possible transition to the withering away of the Communist State. These were the problems which Khrushchev and Tito had promised to try to solve in common at the party-leadership level.

Meanwhile, however, the Hungarian patriots, the third and most legitimate factor in the contest, were running away with the show to such an extent that the other two interested Powers could not catch up with internal developments. The final defeat of Rákosi came indeed at the hands of those he feared and detested most, the Hungarian intellectuals. When the infection of democratization and revolt spread so far as to reach open defiance by the Writers' Union and the Petöfi circle on 27 June 1956 and extended even into the party newspaper, *Szabad Nep*, which published an article on behalf of the rebellious writers, Rákosi realized that he had to act at once against the entire movement. In a resolution of 30 June 1956 of the Central Committee he denounced the Writers' Union, the Union of Working Youth, the Petöfi circle and Imre Nagy and stated that the open opposition to the régime was organized mainly by a group centred around Nagy. He planned to make massive arrests, and Nagy and four hundred others were placed on his lists. Nagy was expelled from the party.

But within two weeks the Soviet leaders realized that Rákosi had lost the power to carry out his belated *coup*. On 11 July, Mikoyan arrived in Budapest. On 18 July a resolution of the Hungarian Central Committee released Rákosi from his post. A new Central Committee was elected, containing people who, like Kádár, Kállaj and Marosan, had been kept in prison by Rákosi. Ernö Gerö was elected in his place. The third phase was opening.

(c) Revolution triumphant

Gerö's election was made without Tito's consent. 'The Russian leaders,' he said in the speech of 11 November 1956, 'made it a condition that Rákosi would go only if Gerö remained. And this was a mistake, because Gerö differed in no way from Rákosi. When we were in the Crimea [Khrushchev went to Yugoslavia on 19 September 1956 and Tito to the Crimea on 27 September] Gerö "happened" to be there and we "accidentally" met him. We talked. He heaped ashes on his head. We wanted to prove that we were not vindictive and so we agreed to have talks with Gerö and a delegation of the Hungarian Workers' Party which was to come to Yugoslavia.' But clearly this was done only to establish a *modus vivendi*. The right man with the right policies was still to be found. Even if Tito had trusted Nagy – and it is still a moot point whether he ever did so – it was clear that the Soviet leadership disapproved of him from the beginning, for otherwise he would at once have been taken back into the party and into the Central Committee. (This happened later, but only under pressure from without.) Thus, with the Russians distrusting Nagy and the Yugoslavs distrusting Gerö, only a third man could ultimately have provided a compromise. This was to be János Kádár.*

* With the benefit of hindsight one can understand more clearly now Kádár's rapid ascent to the task of forming not only, and not primarily, a revisionist Government, but a revisionist party. On 18 July he was elected to the Central Committee and to the Politburo, and made Secretary of the Central Committee. On 9 September, busy as he undoubtedly was, he left for Pekin to attend the sessions of the Eighth Plenum of the Chinese party

But at the time even Tito, like all the Communist leaders in Soviet Russia, still hoped that by appointing Gerö as the new General Secretary the process of de-Stalinization carried out by this former Stalinist would have an immediately appeasing effect on the irate nation. Gerö dismissed the hated General Farkas, the head of the secret police. In an August resolution of the Central Committee on the problems of the intelligentsia, he promised to let the intellectuals have more freedom of action, produce their own work as they wished and get their information and background material at sources of their choice. But already in September the Hungarian intellectuals were again holding protest meetings against the bureaucratic narrow-mindedness of the party. At the end of September the party

(which Ochab also attended in similarly dramatic conditions). On 7 October, the day after the funeral of Rajk in Budapest, which was another milestone of the revolution, Kádár was in Moscow, where he saw Mikoyan and Suslov. On 15 October, he accompanied Gerö to Belgrade where, according to some reports, he impressed Tito more favourably than any other member of the Hungarian delegation. It was at this meeting that, according to Marosan, Tito and the Yugoslavs insisted that the Hungarians should establish Workers' Councils. On 25 October Gerö disappeared for ever, allegedly assassinated by the revolutionaries, and Kádár took his place as First Secretary. On 28 October, Kádár was made the chairman of the Party Presidium of which Nagy (meanwhile rehabilitated) was again a member. On 1 November 1956, on the very day on which the insurrection broke out, he announced the formation of a new party, the Hungarian Socialist Workers' Party, which would see that 'Rákosite despotism is not replaced by the reign of the counter-revolution' and that 'foreign armed intervention would be prevented from allotting to Hungary the tragic fate of Korea'. On 3 November it was announced that all the Communist members of the Nagy Government had resigned with the exception of Kádár and Losonczy. But on 4 November, Kádár appointed himself Prime Minister. This biographical sketch, with its bee-line ascent from relative obscurity to sole command, should of course be seen against the background of Hungarian developments in those vital weeks. In a way all Kádár's moves in his progress towards the leadership were also a desperate uphill fight. As the party itself was slowly sinking under the pressure of the revolution, Kádár's ascent was in a sense an optical illusion: he rose when the party was falling. But when all is said and done it has now emerged more clearly that Kádár believed that he was the one who was destined to save and reform the party from within; and only after he had done that could he proceed with the reconstruction of the Hungarian people's democracy as well. Instructed to sink or swim with the party, he linked his fate to it and did his best to show that he would be worthy of the mission.

started to speak of Nagy's readmission (a development encouraged by the behaviour of the Polish party towards Gomulka). Also by the end of September the Central Council of the Hungarian Trade Unions announced the setting-up of Workers' Councils and of other measures meant to ensure the autonomy of workers' self-government. On 3 October, under mounting pressure, the party announced that the last respects would be paid to 'the victims of Rákosi's despotism'. On 6 October the gruesome reinterment of Rajk and other victims took place.

These episodes did not fail to produce the electrifying and somewhat hysterical effects such occasions can have on excited crowds. On 4 October Imre Nagy asked to be reinstated in the party. On 13 October, this was done. On 14 October Gerö and Kádár left for Yugoslavia, but on 17 October and 20 October the Petöfi circle held three huge meetings in Budapest and on 20 October the offensive mood culminated in the publication by the party organization of the Writers' Union of a resolution calling for a new party congress; the resolution also demanded that Nagy should be consulted on all these matters. On 23 October Tito agreed to sign a communiqué in which the Yugoslav and Hungarian parties pledged themselves to 'devote special attention to promoting mutual relations between the two countries'. But, as he said later, 'matters had already gone pretty far, *a fact which we did not know*, so that Gerö coming to Yugoslavia and our joint declaration could no longer help.'

When Gerö returned from Yugoslavia, on 23 October, events in Hungary developed at breakneck speed. As the Hungarian Press published the full text of Gomulka's statement of 20 October the university students announced that they would hold 'a silent demonstration of sympathy' at the Polish Embassy on the same day. At noon the Minister of the Interior announced the banning of the demonstration. Two hours later the demonstration was allowed to take place. By 3 o'clock two hundred thousand demonstrators, mostly young people, were marching in both parts of Budapest, chanting Petöfi's verse, 'We will never again be slaves.' In the evening Gerö spoke to the nation on the radio, addressing himself particularly to the

workers, and asking them to be patient and give the party time
to implement the measures it wanted to take.

But as he was speaking the scenes in the street were taking on
a revolutionary character. The Parliament, the Hungarian radio
and the printing press of *Szabad Nep* were under siege. The
premises of the newspaper were seriously damaged. At 10.20
p.m. a Central Committee meeting was held. It was then that
Nagy was allegedly appointed Prime Minister, for immediately
afterwards orders and declarations signed by him were posted.
Yet Nagy learned of his appointment only late the next day.
(In an interview on 31 October 1956 with the Austrian radio
station he said that 'later on, after two or three days, I was made
Premier and the people were unable to differentiate'.) Among
the documents allegedly signed by Nagy in these first days there
figured on the morning of 24 October 1956 the appeal by the
Hungarian Government for Soviet military assistance. Nagy
later vehemently denied that he ever signed such a document,
and went on to say that he had not even been informed of his
appointment. It is very probable then that Gerö, and the other
Hungarian Stalinists advised by the Russians, announced his
appointment primarily because they were going in any case to
ask for Soviet intervention.*

The request on 24 October for help 'in accordance with the
terms of the Warsaw Treaty of the Soviet formations stationed
in Hungary' is of particular significance in the history of the
Hungarian revolution. The fact that the Hungarian Communists
called for help in such an ignominious way showed how serious
the situation in the country had become. The gloomy assessment by the Hungarian Communist Party and very probably by
its Soviet advisers of the party's power in the country and its

---

* This was one of the three particularly infamous actions in this dramatic
story in which both the Hungarian Communists and the Russians behaved
with such cruelty and felony. The other two were: the arrest in the building
of the Soviet Command in Budapest of the Hungarian military emissaries
headed by General Pál Maléter, who had gone to discuss on the eve of
4 November the procedure for the withdrawal of Soviet troops; and Imre
Nagy's arrest and kidnapping as he was leaving the Yugoslav Embassy,
where he had taken refuge on 4 November and whence he had been released
on the assurance of a full Hungarian safe-conduct.

probably have headed the Government for a shorter
riod of transition. It remained to be seen what form
ngary would have adopted : a people's democracy, a
nocracy, a parliamentary democracy?

this was clear, the problem of the actual future of
as now transferred to the international plane. Would
ia occupy Hungary in order to keep her within her
nd in this case would the West react, and how?
re be a war and would Hungary, as Kádár had
come another Korea?

ese questions were being considered, the entire
the future of the revolution was rapidly becoming an
al question. By 30 October Socialist Revolutionary
om all parts of the country were scaling down their
nds to 'the immediate withdrawal from the Warsaw
the immediate recall of all Soviet troops', as well as –
a new point – asking 'the United Nations to deal
with the case of Hungary in as much as the inter-
the Soviet troops had made an international issue of
al affairs'. On 31 October Nagy had announced that:
we opened negotiations for the withdrawal of Soviet
n the country and for the renunciation of our obliga-
ming from the Warsaw Treaty.' On 1 November he
gram to Voroshilov, the Chairman of the Supreme
king for the withdrawal of Soviet troops from
nd on the same day he informed Hammarskjöld, the
General of the United Nations, officially that he had
to the Soviet Ambassador against the entry of further
ts into Hungary and also that he had, as head of the
Government, unilaterally repudiated the Warsaw
d declared Hungary's neutrality. He now asked to
uestion of Hungary's neutrality put on the agenda of
Nations and 'for the help of the four Great Powers
ng the country's neutrality'. At this point on 1 Novem-
ommunist ministers left the Cabinet. Once Hungary
liated the Warsaw Treaty and declared its neutrality
as at Khrushchev's feet.

October, the Soviet Government had issued a declara-

chances of maintaining order led them to take this step. In fact, the balance was already broken when they appealed on 24 October for foreign military help. Tito's theory, in his speech of 11 November, on this particular point, namely that while the first demand for intervention on 24 October was wrong and immoral, the second on 4 November, made by Kádár, was justified because the 'Fascist counter-revolution had to be crushed', is equivocal. It is true to say that the premature demand for foreign intervention exacerbated the outraged population even more. Indeed, ever since 24 October the main question debated by the Hungarian revolutionaries was that of 'the withdrawal from the Warsaw Treaty', under the provisions of which the demand had been made, and its corollary: the problem of neutrality. This was Nagy's main mandate from the Hungarian people; the rest was secondary. It might also be true to say, as Tito does, that while the first insurgent crowds were 'mostly Communists and youth, who could have been treated by other means than Soviet tanks', the enormously swollen crowds gathering not only in Budapest but later in every town and village in Hungary were indeed of a different kind, size and force, and the remnants of the former Hungarian Communist army and police could do nothing against them. But the theory does not hold water because, in principle, to ask for foreign intervention is either admissible or inadmissible, whatever the circumstances (and indeed nothing lowered Tito's prestige in Eastern Europe more than his embarrassed condoning of the second Russian intervention); and because such was the impetus of events that very probably even if Nagy and Kádár had come effectively to power on 24 October and had not asked for Soviet troops, the irresistible transformation of the initial demands for reforms into a claim for total national emancipation would still have followed. In other words, after 24 October there was no other way for a Communist Government to maintain itself in power in Hungary than by the active backing of the Soviet army.

On 25 October the Government announced that the counter-revolutionary 'putsch' had been suppressed by 'the forces of internal security and the units of the fraternal Soviet army'. On 25 October Imre Nagy also announced that his Government would initiate negotiations about the withdrawal of Soviet forces stationed in Hungary, and Kádár asked for time and patience. The same day the popular secretary of the Petöfi circle, Gabor Tanczos, appealed for the restoration of order. But it was of no avail. The movement was now spreading all over the country and particularly rapidly in the villages, whence it was going to boomerang to the capital. On 26 October Workers' Councils were set up in Csepel and other places. At the same time, the Central Committee of the Hungarian Workers' Party made known the new series of reforms which it was preparing: the formation of a new Government on the broadest national foundations; negotiations for complete equality between Hungary and the Soviet Union; approval of Workers' Councils in the factories but through the intermediary of the trade union organs; amnesty; and a broad programme of 'social democracy'. On 27 October the Central Council of the Trade Unions proclaimed that 'the wish of the working class has been realized: enterprises will be managed by workers' councils.' The same day a new Government was formed with Nagy as Prime Minister and mostly Communist ministers with the exception of the two venerable members of the Smallholders' Party: Zoltán Tildy and Béla Kovács. On 28 October Nagy presented his Government and his programme by radio to the people; and Kádár announced the dissolution of the old party organs and the setting-up of the new praesidium with himself as Chairman. But already on 28 October the flames of the revolution which had spread now to all the corners of the country were rushing back like a forest fire towards Budapest.

What had happened was that in the countryside, where there were no Soviet forces and where the local security forces and the party apparatus had been incapacitated, if not liquidated, by the insurgents, institutions such as Workers' Councils, students' parliaments, and socialist revolutionary councils were spontaneously formed by the people, and were defining the policy which they thought the Government should follow. Their demands were usually: general and free elections to be held within two months with the participation of several parties; 'the immediate recall of Soviet troops from our country, not to their

bases, but to their fatherland,
tion of the security police; an
Szabad Nep itself published a
Pravda on the situation in Hu
Anti-Popular Adventure in Hu
the paper. 'What happened i
popular nor an adventure. Wh
On 29 October it was officially
were withdrawing from Budape
October there were still units in
contradictory reports came fr
Soviet units pouring into Hu
announced the restoration of t
formation of a coalition Govern
Social-Democratic, Smallholders
'like in 1945'.

(d) The Soviet intervention

The fourth phase of the story h
ing-point 30 October, because on
the entire problem of the Hungar
from the national to the internati
purposes the revolution in Hung
framework was finished by 30 Oc
anti-Communist forces. The fact
longer commanded either the arr
therefore lay open to the mour
population was reflected in the c
ment and of political structure w
Hungary was again, on paper, a
system. Elections, which were goi
sible, would have undoubtedly re
the Communists. The re-establish
order would have followed, in wh
changes which took place during
been institutionalized: the setting-
and the disbanding of the collective
by the people for his stand, but no

tion 'on the principles of development and further strengthening of friendship and cooperation between the Soviet Union and other Socialist States'. This declaration is one of the basic texts for the understanding of the Soviet attitude on this issue after the Twentieth Congress. It was, of course, issued for *ad hoc* purposes and actually contained a second part dealing specifically with the situation in Hungary and hypocritically regretting 'the bloodshed which occurred in Hungary and assuring the Hungarian Government that it had given its military command instructions to withdraw the Soviet military units from the city of Budapest as soon as this would be considered necessary by the Hungarian Government.' The operative expression was 'the Hungarian Government'. The next day the Communists left the Nagy Government in order to try to form a rival one of their own. But in its general philosophy the Soviet document propounded a new definition of relationships within the Soviet bloc which met with the approval of Gomulka, Tito and Mao. The expression 'socialist commonwealth' was introduced, thus making a deliberate attempt to erase the memories of Stalin's empire. The document duly recognized 'the downright mistakes, violations and errors which disfigured the principle of equality in relations among the socialist States', and showed that the Twentieth Congress of the CPSU had already, and resolutely, condemned them. The Soviet Government was pledging itself to strengthen from then on its friendship and cooperation with the other socialist countries on the firm foundation of the observance of the full sovereignty of each Socialist State. It made the point that this included the economic sphere, in which further strengthening of economic ties was forecast (and COMECON was soon after that put on a new footing). It announced the recall, when feasible, of the Soviet advisers.

In the military domain the Soviet Government described the Warsaw Treaty as the 'basis of the mutual relations between the Soviet Union and the peoples' democracies', acknowledged the presence of Soviet troops in Rumania, Hungary and Poland according to the Warsaw Treaty and other agreements, and went farther, announcing its readiness 'to review with the other socialist countries which are members of the Warsaw

Treaty the question of Soviet troops stationed in their territories'.

As a general text, therefore, the document makes it clear that provided a country was considered by the Soviet Union to be socialist, a people's democracy and a loyal member of the Warsaw Treaty, the Soviet Union was prepared to treat it as a sovereign country, which meant that it could build socialism in whatever national form it chose. On the special point of Hungary, the fact that Nagy himself announced the next day the repudiation of the Warsaw Treaty and the formation of a democratic and not a socialist Government did not change the Soviet attitude or plans. If and when the Soviet Union intervened she would do so on the basis of some formal demand from a Communist Government, located on Hungarian territory or even from without. The delay in deciding on intervention was due much more to international factors than to internal ones.

On 30 October the Anglo–French ultimatum to Egypt on the question of the Suez Canal was issued. This threw the entire Western world and the United States into an even greater turmoil than that provoked by the Hungarian crisis. The military operations in the Suez Canal lasted more than two weeks. The relations between the United States and Great Britain and France were unprecedentedly strained. In both Great Britain and France public opinion was bitterly divided. In New York, the debates on the Suez question and on the Hungarian question kept the United Nations in a state of constant alert.

On 3 November at 10 p.m. Pál Maléter, the Defence Minister, Kovács, the Chief of the General Staff, and the other members of the Hungarian delegation sent to discuss the technical conditions of the withdrawal of the Soviet troops entered the building of the Soviet Army Headquarters and never came back. On 4 November Imre Nagy announced over the radio that the Soviet troops had launched an air attack on Budapest. On 4 November Kádár announced the formation of his rival Government which had 'requested the command of the Soviet army to help our nation in smashing the sinister forces of reaction'. He also sent a telegram to the United Nations asking that the question of Hungary be withdrawn from the agenda. The Soviet guns then opened up in Budapest and Soviet troops and armoured cars were soon in action in the whole country. Through the open frontier with Austria, hundreds of thousands of freedom fighters fled to the West. Those who remained in the country were either killed in action against the Soviet tanks or were arrested and later executed or jailed by the security troops which were re-formed with Soviet, Rumanian and Czechoslovak help. The Hungarian people, workers, youth, intellectuals, farmers, who had responded so spontaneously to the first hope of national emancipation, were afflicted by a deep historic trauma. In the Communist world there started what André Malraux has called, in another context, '*le temps du mépris*', a time of shame.

The Hungarian revolution left the main questions of Russia's new form of rule in Eastern Europe wide open, gaping like Budapest's main buildings, their façades demolished by the Soviet shells.

It left open the question of neutrality, the public demand for which had been silenced only by Soviet intervention. But the question sank deeply into the political consciousness of all Communist and non-Communist Eastern Europeans, and flares up as the main question whenever the future of the Eastern European countries is seriously discussed.

It left open the question of national Communism, the conflict of influence between Tito and Khrushchev. In spite of the fact that Tito approved grudgingly of the Soviet intervention and in spite of the fact that Khrushchev endorsed the Yugoslav way of building socialism, the aspiration towards national Communism remained a deep reality in the politics of Eastern Europe.

It left open the question of the prestige and authority of the Soviet Union in Eastern Europe. Twice already since Stalin's death, to maintain their power his successors had had to use Soviet tanks against workers and revolutionaries in countries within his empire. But the prestige and the authority of the Soviet Union, already damaged by Tito's victory, sank even lower.

It left open the question of how much control and influence the CPSU can maintain over the world Communist movement.

For, no sooner had the opposition of right-wing national Communists and revisionists been stilled by compromise and violent ideological adjustments than a new attack was launched against the CPSU leadership from the opposite quarter: the left-wing dogmatists. To this we now turn.

3 The Dogmatists (1958-63)

(i) The protagonists

The second setback to the authority of the Russian Communists came at the hands of the Albanian and Chinese parties. Once more the hegemony of the CPSU was openly challenged. Once more the battle between the parties developed into a battle between the States ruled by the warring parties, with all the diplomatic strains and subtleties of protocol which this entails. Once more the Russians tried the only solution possible in such cases: to remove and chastise the rebellious leaders of the parties which challenged theirs – and once more they failed. Once more the Russian leader who had been responsible for a major political defeat disappeared from the political stage at the moment when defeat had been conceded: Stalin had died a timely death, Khrushchev was deposed (whether too soon or too late remains to be seen).

The attack of the left-wing Albanian and Chinese parties on Khrushchev follows logically as well as chronologically upon the victory of the right-wing revisionists, headed by the Yugoslavs. This is because, in the first place, the initial defeat gave new courage to the other parties which for different, or even opposite, reasons wanted to free themselves from the CPSU's leadership. In the second place it is only natural – dialectic, the Communists would say – that once the opposition from the right had won a victory, the opposition from the left would be even more determined to assert its own point of view. When the centre of power is stable, it may expect to have to repress two or more contrary trends from opposite directions. But when the centre cannot hold, the wings fall apart. The more Khrushchev absorbed revisionism into official Communist doctrine as upheld by the CPSU, as the maker of doctrine, the more it antagonized the dogmatist parties or leaders. The first Chinese accusations were hurled against the Yugoslavs only; and whenever during the first years Khrushchev criticized them personally and on behalf of the world Communist movement, he received due praise and backing from the Chinese. But when, after 1960, Khrushchev pointedly avoided criticizing the Yugoslavs in public, and later condoned publicly their 'way of building socialism', the Chinese decided to launch their overall attack against the Yugoslavs and the Russians together. Thirdly, the Albanian entry into the conflict on the Chinese side was a logical consequence of Khrushchev's *rapprochement* with Tito. For the Albanians the acid test of a party's friendship or enmity was its attitude to Tito, and the fact that the Chinese concentrated their doctrinal attacks on the Yugoslavs endeared them greatly to the Albanians. This is what brought them into the conflict and made the duel a fourfold one, in which, as Edward Crankshaw said, Khrushchev and Mao were sticking pins in the hearts of Hoxha and Tito respectively in the hope that they would pierce the hearts of Khrushchev and Mao.

But speaking strictly chronologically, neither the Sino–Soviet nor the Albanian–Yugoslav conflicts originated in 1958 nor do they end with Khrushchev's fall in 1964. This must be made clear lest readers might be led to believe that the switching of this survey from the revisionists to the dogmatists and then to the neutralists corresponds exactly with clear-cut phases. The CPSU is today engaged simultaneously in competition with the Yugoslavs on the question of ideological influence in Eastern Europe; in a struggle with the Chinese for the hegemony of the world Communist movement; and is on the defensive against the 'polycentric' neutralists, the number of which is growing so rapidly. Thus all three trends, although in many ways originating from each other, have a parallel history.

The conflict between Communist China and the USSR started implicitly and almost inevitably when Mao and his team seized power in the entire mainland of China in 1949. Explicitly, the leadership of the CCP made it unmistakably clear after their coming to power that, while they acknowledged the seniority of the CPSU, they would accept its theses only when and if they were correct from a Marxist–Leninist point of view, as interpreted by the Chinese. Mao's early slogan of 'let a hundred flowers bloom' implied that flowers do not bloom in the shadow, in anybody's shadow; and the five points proposed by the Chinese at the Bandung Conference all stressed the right of any Communist country to national sovereignty, political independence and ideological autonomy. As two neighbouring Powers, China and Russia had old and difficult accounts to settle: the problem of frontier adjustment, of the status of Inner Mongolia and Manchuria, as well as of brotherly economic and military relations. As two Communist parties, their relations were fundamentally affected by the memory of the fact that, in 1946, it was by refusing to follow Stalin's advice that the Chinese won their final and complete political and national victory; and in 1927, when they had followed Stalin's advice, they had been betrayed by him to Chiang Kai-shek, who afterwards smashed the entire Chinese party. Only Mao's group escaped, by taking to the mountains. (Mao was quite right to protest in his polemics with Khrushchev against the epithet 'Stalinist' with which his party was labelled.) Thus the roots of the Sino–Soviet conflict strike down very deeply into the past history of the two parties and countries.

Similarly the conflict between the Albanian and Yugoslav parties started as early as 1944, when it became clear that the Albanian party was deeply split between the pro-Western and anti-Yugoslav group led by Hoxha and the group led by Xoxe, which was not only obviously under Tito's spell, but advocated the merging of Albania with Yugoslavia. The Yugoslav–Soviet dispute in 1948 gave Hoxha the opportunity to order a complete purge in the ranks of the Albanian party – starting with Xoxe, who was executed. Since then, the Albanian party's hatred of the Yugoslavs has become the mainspring of all their political actions and when in 1960 they were convinced that Khrushchev was favourably inclined towards Yugoslavia, they did not hesitate to be the first to attack him openly. As a neighbouring country, Albania. fears Yugoslavia's historical tendency to absorb her into the Yugoslav Federal Republic; she resents Yugoslav 'Great Power chauvinism' which prevents Albania from reincorporating the northern province of the Kosmet, which she had coveted since 1921; and she objected to Yugoslav economic exploitation in the form of joint Yugoslav–Albanian mixed companies (on the Soviet model, which Yugoslavia afterwards denounced as an imperialist Soviet institution) or by means of economic and trade relations. The Albanian attitude towards Soviet Russia is conditioned by the Russian attitude towards Yugoslavia.

The causes of this quadrilateral conflict are so deep and irreconcilable, and go so far back in history, that it is understandable that it cannot be solved in 1964 by the mere removal of one person, Nikita Sergeyievich Khrushchev, from the scene. Here again the story will go on unfolding long after the events outlined here. At present all that can be attempted is to retrace the three separate trends in the conflict. Those are: first, the abstract and general ideological opposition between the dogmatists and the revisionists (pp. 90–102); second, the growth of the more practical differences between the Chinese Communists and the CPSU (pp. 102–7); and third, the evolution of the relations between the Albanian Communists and the Yugoslav and Soviet parties (pp. 107–12); and then to describe how between 1960 and 1964 these three original conflicts grew into the dispute which shook the entire Communist world.

(ii) The ideological issue

With some risk of over-simplification, the complex of ideological positions and almost temperamental attitudes which separate a dogmatist party, group or even individual from a revisionist party, group or individual can be broadly classified in three main issues:

(*a*) the issue of the overall leadership, discipline, and solidarity of the Communist movement;

(*b*) the issue of Communist strategy; and

(*c*) the issue of the differing economic standards between one Communist state and another.*

* See Alexander Dallin: *Diversity in International Communism* (Columbia University Press, 1963), which contains a more complete account of the issues at stake and of the alternative solutions proposed by the two camps.

(a) The 'general line'

Although the three issues are of equal importance and are deeply interlocked with each other, the right of the CPSU to claim the leadership of the entire Communist movement stands out as the first and touchiest question of all. This right, historically, had not been called in question since the foundation of the Communist International in March 1919, when Lenin overruled all previous objections to the fact that the CPSU might control too closely the work of the other parties. Since then, the CPSU, as the only party in power, has been able to direct through corruption and organizational subversion all the Communist parties which are in opposition in their own countries. Under Stalin, the International itself was made an agent of Soviet foreign policy. Dissolved just before the Second World War, the International never reappeared – and it could not reappear, because after the Second World War the basic conditions which had given the CPSU such an easy run had changed: there were other Communist Parties in power in other countries, three of which had come to power by their own means and strength: the Yugoslav, the Albanian and the Chinese, which, in this chronological order, questioned the infallibility of the CPSU's rule. Stalin's attempt in 1947 to re-establish control over the ruling parties through the Cominform was short-lived.

The reconsideration of the entire question of collaboration between the 'fraternal parties' was in the offing. This was carried out on four separate occasions: at the Twentieth Congress of the CPSU in February 1956; at the November 1957 Moscow meeting of the ruling Communist parties, which issued a common declaration; at the January 1959 Twenty-First Congress of the CPSU and at the 1960 November meeting of the Eighty-One Communist Parties. At all these meetings, compromise solutions were worked out in order to find a common 'general line'. This was of no avail. In the absence of a unified central command, the resolutions of goodwill went by the board, and while the dogmatists upheld some paragraphs and chapters in which their own views had been incorporated, the revisionists invoked the other paragraphs, inserted at their request.

In the accompanying discussion, it became only too clear that the split went deep. While the revisionists were in principle more inclined to argue that several centres of Communist leadership should coexist together (for which the Italian leader Togliatti coined the expression 'polycentrism'), the dogmatists, headed by the Chinese Communist Party, insisted that there should be a binding ideology for all parties. The Chinese and the other dogmatist parties were dissatisfied with the line taken by the CPSU after the Twentieth Congress, and especially after the Twenty-Second. And, as we have seen (on p. 58), they were more eager than many other parties, and especially Governments, to have a Communist 'general line' established, as they felt it could be made to reflect their own needs and views. It would, they said, be 'liquidationist' for them to renounce such a line and the doctrine that some common Communist organization should uphold and control it. The fact that the present line was unsatisfactory and that the CPSU, as its upholder, was mistaken, did not alter the Chinese view on the need for a common doctrine and leadership. The most striking demonstration of this dogmatist attitude occurred in the period between 1956 and 1959 when the Chinese, fearful of the current of 'polycentrism' in the world Communist movement and especially in Europe and Eastern Europe, militated strongly for the acknowledgement of the CPSU's leadership in the Communist movement. They were quite clear that they preferred a unity dominated by Russia to no unity at all. This attitude should be compared with, for instance, Togliatti's revisionist report of 10 November 1961:

Certainly we cannot deny that this way of acting of ours has given our party a particular, original stamp in the very extensive camp of the international communist movement of today. But this does not at all disturb us – quite the contrary. We have persistently advocated for quite a long time now that the struggle of the working class and the vanguard party of the working class [in each country] must have a stamp of its own, corresponding to the conditions and traditions of the country and a corresponding course of political action. It is for that reason that we valued so much the decisions of the Twentieth Congress, especially the affirmation of the political and organizational autonomy of every communist party. . . . The widespread nature of the communist movement in countries far from one another, the diversity of actual conditions and the inevitable diversity of political action and working methods make it necessary to have this multiplicity of directing centres.

This leads us to a consideration of the relevance of Soviet experiences to the ideological evolution of the other parties (the relevance of the Soviet experience to the building of socialism in other countries is discussed separately on pp. 99–102). Because Soviet evolution had been directed for thirty years by Stalin, this is tantamount to discussing his influence and the cult of personality – as denounced by the Twentieth Congress. An article by Oskar Lange in *Politika* of 2 December 1961 gives the characteristic attitude of the East European revisionists:

As Marxists we know that the phenomenon of the personality cult cannot be reduced solely to the problem of one man's character, or that of a small group of people. We deal here with a social phenomenon, which demands a Marxist analysis. Comrade Gomulka presented an outline of such an analysis in his speech, indicating how the phenomenon of Stalin's personality cult originated in the specific historical conditions of the Soviet Union. . . . We still lack a clear picture of what the other alternatives were and why they were not chosen. This is a difficult and complicated matter; its analysis will require time. This task belongs, first of all, to the Soviet comrades. It is not exclusively a problem of satisfying our theoretical curiosity: the whole international workers' movement needs such an analysis for practical reasons. The phenomenon of the personality cult and everything linked with it is not an inevitable state through which all countries and especially underdeveloped countries must pass in the process of building socialism.

The attitude of the dogmatists on the other hand was to endorse Stalin's major achievements in building the first socialist State. The Chinese article entitled 'On the Question of Stalin' of 13 September 1963 reads:

In defending Stalin, the Chinese Communist Party defends the correct side, defends the glorious history of the struggle of the first state of the dictatorship of the proletariat, which was created by the October revolution; it defends the glorious history of the struggle of the CPSU; it defends the prestige of the international communist movement among working people throughout the world. In brief, it defends the theory and practice of Marxism–Leninism.

The following passage, from an Albanian article of 2 November 1961 (bearing the characteristic title 'The name and deeds of Josif Vissarionovich Stalin live and will live for centuries to come'), makes the attitude of the dogmatists even clearer on this issue:

J. V. Stalin devoted his whole life to the great cause of the revolution, to the liberation of the exploited, to socialism and communism. The open struggle against J. V. Stalin is a struggle against his immortal deeds, a struggle against Marxism–Leninism.

Finally, linked directly with the issue of the 'general line', there arises the question of whether parties whose lines 'might be interpreted differently' really belong to the 'Communist family of parties'. Here both revisionists and dogmatists show a very pragmatic point of view. The parties of which each of them approved were considered to belong; and each of them demanded vehemently that the parties of which they disapproved should be eliminated from the community. Here is a telling passage from the CCP statement on the 'general line' of 14 June 1963 already mentioned. 'How to treat the Marxist–Leninist fraternal Albanian Party of Labour is one question. How to treat the Yugoslav revisionist clique of traitors to Marxism–Leninism is quite another question.' The same point of view, in reverse, was proclaimed by the CPSU when it caused the Albanians to be eliminated from the 'family' and wooed the Yugoslavs to return whole-heartedly to it.

This led to another controversial distinction: that of the 'objective membership' of a fraternal party. For the dogmatists, as well as for a great many other Communist parties, the Albanians, even if ostracized, continued to belong to the Communist camp, for the objective reason that because even if one did not approve of the way that they were building socialism, one had however to acknowledge that they *were* building socialism. This idea of 'objective membership' had arisen as a result of Stalin's failure to eliminate the Yugoslavs once and for all. Communist parties had become sceptical about Moscow's ability to carry out such excommunications, and what they had felt secretly about the Yugoslavs during the years in which Stalin forced all parties to turn their backs on them they could now express more or less openly when Khrushchev attempted to wipe out with his individual excommunication an entire Communist party and country.

The fundamental question was thus that of deciding what the 'general line' contained and by whom it should be administered. Broadly speaking, the revisionists by their admission of 'polycentrism' implicitly take a milder view of the binding nature of one single dogma. They doubt its capacity to embrace the diversity of all aspects of Communist problems, and they question the wisdom of having one authority to dispense guidance and judgement. The dogmatists, and especially the Chinese, uphold the necessity of having one single collective authority and one fully accepted doctrine worked out on the basis of consultations between parties. What they thought this doctrine should be and by whom it should be administered they made forcibly clear in the stream of articles and statements before the break, and in the recapitulations they have provided ever since.

(b) Communist strategy in the nuclear age

This is the issue about which most is known in the West. Most Westerners do actually think that the whole conflict amounts to a divergence on revolutionary strategy or even more simply on relations with the capitalist West. Khrushchev as the peaceful statesman and Mao as the war-mongering revolutionary were the symbols of the conflict in the eyes of the non-Communist world.

In a very simplified version this is not so far from the truth. As far as Communist world strategy is concerned the main policies of Mao and the Chinese remained very much what they were in 1946, when Stalin and Zhdanov reasserted the basic irreconcilability of the two worlds – one doomed and declining rapidly, the other with total victory already within its grasp. The grandiose enlargement of the Communist dominion on the map of the world was a sign of the rapidity of this victory. The emancipation of the colonial peoples was the proof of the irreversible trend against the capitalist-colonial West. The possession of the nuclear bomb by the West did not alter the basic premise – for in Mao's conception battles were won by human masses, which could not all be destroyed by bombs; and its possession by Soviet Russia brought him to the conclusion that the moment had come for the great Communist offensive.

In the meantime, though, the CPSU under Khrushchev's leadership undertook to revise the Marxist–Leninist–Stalinist doctrine in the light of new conditions. In their eyes radically new conditions had been created by the three main phenomena of the aftermath of the Second World War: the territorial advance of Communism, the dissolution of the colonial empires and nuclear warfare.

From this reconsideration by Russia, there sprang the great argument, the most heated of the entire controversy, on the strategy of the world Communist movement. While the Russian positions became more flexible and were therefore treated as 'revisionist', the Chinese found every reason in the new analysis to stiffen and exacerbate the old claims and therefore were described as 'dogmatist'.

This aspect of the dispute is already well known, but it can be briefly and very clearly studied in the following two comprehensive summaries by each of the leading protagonists.

The Russian view is best summed up in a list of subjects for consideration sent by the Central Committee of the CPSU to the Central Committee of the CPS of 30 March 1963:

(a) Questions concerning the struggle for the further strengthening of the might of the world socialist system. The transformation into the decisive factor in the development of human society, which is the main distinguishing feature of our era.

(*b*) Questions concerning the struggle for peace and peaceful co-existence. The need to pool the efforts of all peace-loving forces for the struggle to prevent a world thermo-nuclear war. The creation and the strengthening of the broadcast united front of peace supporters. The exposure of the reactionary essence of imperialism, the heightening of vigilance and the mobilization of the broad masses to fight against the preparations being made by the imperialists for a new world war, to frustrate their aggressive schemes and to isolate the forces of reaction and war. Assertion in international relations of the Leninist principle of peaceful coexistence between states with different social systems. The struggle for general disarmament and for the elimination of the traces of the Second World War.

(*c*) Questions concerning the struggle against imperialism headed by the US. The utilization, in the interests of our camp, of the weaknesses of imperialism and the growing impotence of the entire capitalist system of world economy. The aggravation of the contradictions of capitalism, especially those between labour and capital, and the aggravation of the severe crisis in bourgeois ideology and politics. Support of the revolutionary and class struggle of the working people in the capitalist countries against the monopolies, for their social liberation, for the abolition of the exploitation of man by man, for the extension of the democratic rights and freedoms of the people.

(*d*) Questions concerning the national-liberation movement. The support and utmost development of the national-liberation movement of the peoples. The struggle for the complete and final ending of colonialism and neo-colonialism in all its forms. The rendering of support to peoples fighting against colonialism and also to countries which have achieved their national liberation. The development of economic and cultural cooperation with their countries.

This formulation, with its stress on peaceful coexistence, was rejected by the dogmatists, headed by the CCP, as both false in its valuation and wrong in the order of priority it gave to the various problems facing Communist strategy in the world. In the five points of the CCP's proposal of 14 June 1963 concerning the general line the 'erroneous views' of the CPSU were summarized.

(*a*) The view which blots out the class content of the contradiction between the socialist and imperialist camps and fails to see this contradiction as one between states under the dictatorship of the

E

proletariat and states under the dictatorship of the monopoly of the capitalists;

(*b*) the view which recognizes only the contradiction between the socialist and the imperialist camps while neglecting or underestimating the contradiction between the proletariat and the bourgeoisie in the capitalist world, between the oppressed nations and imperialism, among the imperialist countries and among the monopoly capitalist groups, and the struggles to which the contradictions give rise;

(*c*) the view which maintains with regard to the capitalist world that the contradictions between the proletariat and the bourgeoisie can be solved without a proletarian revolution in each country and that the contradiction between the oppressed nations and imperialism can be resolved without revolution by the oppressed nations;

(*d*) the view which denies that the development of the inherent contradiction in the contemporary capitalist world inevitably leads to a new situation in which the imperialist countries are locked in an intense struggle and asserts that the contradictions among the imperialist countries can be reconciled or even eliminated, by 'international agreements among the big monopolies'; and

(*e*) the view which maintains that the contradiction between the two world systems of socialism and capitalism will automatically disappear in the course of 'economic competition', that the other fundamental world contradictions will automatically do so with the disappearance of the contradictions between the two systems, and that a world without want, a new world of 'all-round cooperation' will appear.

Each of the five 'erroneous views' corresponds in fact to one of the main points of the Soviet Communist world strategy. At each of the major turning-points in the relations between Soviet Russia and the West – the U-2 incident in April 1960, the Cuban crisis in 1962, and the nuclear test ban treaty in 1963 (all of which form part of the story of this chapter) – Russian policy was criticized by China and the strategic controversy grew ever more stormy. At each of the Communist conferences and congresses which took place between 1960 and 1964 (most of which also form an integral part of this story) the opposing positions were confirmed and strengthened, each of the parties trying to win to their side and to their point of view the other Communist parties.

(c) Equality in the Communist camp

The Communist parties of the world reacted to the main ideological issues of the Soviet and the Chinese debates in different ways. Although a hard-core 'dogmatist' and a hard-core 'revisionist' grouping can always be found, the reaction of the majority of the parties over the period 1960–4 by no means conformed to one single pattern. On the first of the three main issues into which the ideological argument is here divided, the 'general line' issue, it can be said that the Soviet and Chinese parties agreed on the need for a centre and a dogma, while the minor parties were more inclined to see the advantages of polycentrism. On the issue of world Communist strategy, Khrushchev's 'peaceful' policy carried the majority of the senior parties; on the other hand, on the issue of equalizing economic differences the Chinese, as the champions of the 'have-nots', made the strongest impact on the majority of the parties. Generally speaking, they found distasteful and contrary to basic Communist ethics the CPSU's post-Stalinist attitude which favoured a 'Russian affluent Communism' and the perpetuation of the 'inherent differences of level between the various Communist countries'.

Jealousy is one of the driving forces of history – and the idea of historic competition and 'catching-up' inspires Russia's ambitions in the industrial war, especially with regard to the United States. In the same way it inspires the ambitions of China and of all the coloured peoples in relation to the white societies; those of the Eastern European peoples in relation to the Western Europeans; and, finally, at an even deeper level, those of the agricultural Eastern European countries in relation to the industrial ones. It is based on the perennial feeling of national ambition and it is here that the Chinese and the dogmatists drew the deepest cleavage between the Russians and the rest of the Communist parties.

The importance of the issue cannot be overstressed. For it is this general sense of inferiority which gives rise to such different and important points of conflict between the two camps as: the question of the objective stages of socialist evolution; the relevance of Soviet experience in establishing the phases of evolution of a socialist State; the acceptability of short-cuts in this evolution, as for example the Chinese 'leap forward' and the 'agricultural communes'; the difference between 'international socialist economic cooperation' and Great Power chauvinism; the difference between Russia's affluent communism and the Chinese conception of revolutionary austerity; the question of the simultaneous arrival at the final stage of socialism of all the Communist States together; the need for more developed Communist countries to delay their advance so as to be able to help the less developed ones to reach the same economic and technical level – which means sharing with all the other Communist countries the technical discoveries and know-how even in the nuclear field.

The Communist doctrinaire who more than any other emphasized the importance of this basic difference between the two attitudes was Luigi Longo. In his report to the Central Committee of the Italian party of 21–22 December 1961 he drew his colleagues' attention to the fact that 'the disagreement between the Russian and the Chinese parties goes beyond the questions of peaceful coexistence, avoidability of war and cult of personality. At the root of this disagreement there is perhaps a different conception of the march towards socialism and communism of the countries of the socialist system. According to one conception, this march should occur as a single whole; the more advanced countries should set the pace to suit that of the more backward countries, putting all their material advantages at the disposal of the latter to accelerate their march.

'It is clear that such a conception cannot be reconciled with the economic challenge hurled at the capitalist countries by the USSR, with the strategic and tactical position of peaceful coexistence, with foreign economic aid to ex-colonial countries nor even with the programme for the transition to communism and related measures, including the transformation of the dictatorship of the proletariat into an all-people State. The Chinese comrades do not conceal their reservations on this aspect of Soviet policy.'

These different conceptions of the march towards socialism

led to some of the most profound divergencies between the two camps. The idea of 'rhythm of development' was and is constantly invoked by the Russians in Communist, political, technical and economic debates; and so is the idea of 'proletarian international solidarity' by the Chinese. These two slogans were to be heard for instance when Soviet Russia finally abrogated its promise to help China to develop nuclear bombs; or when an abrupt end was also put to Soviet Russia's harassed promise to 'help' the speedy development of China – even at the cost of her own development and internal and external economic policies – so that China could quickly reach a level almost equal to that of Soviet Russia in the technical and military fields. An immediate result of Russia's rebuff was China's launching of more impatient and demanding slogans for the economic levelling of all Communist countries; for massive technical and financial help to be given to anti-colonialist countries, and for political and revolutionary priority to be given to the struggle of the anti-colonial peoples for their 'national-liberation' from beneath the colonialist yoke.

This campaign in its turn led to two undeniable setbacks for Soviet Russia, one in the world at large and one within the Soviet bloc. In general the Chinese demand for direct and practical help to the underdeveloped countries 'on this earth and not in the moon' and for direct revolutionary backing of all insurrectionist movements against the colonialist powers in all continents increased her popularity with the Governments of the underdeveloped countries and with the revolutionary parties of the countries still in a colonial or quasi-colonial status. At the same time the image projected by the Chinese of Soviet Russia as a Super-Power competing peacefully with the other Super-Power, the United States, for advance in space research and for a higher standard of living tarnished Russia's universal prestige as a revolutionary Power. In the Soviet bloc the theme of the 'equalization of economic development' was heard above all in the opposition which the Rumanian Workers' Party conducted, with strong Chinese support, against Khrushchev's policy of transforming COMECON into an East European supra-national organization. This, in turn, started a new centrifugal wave of nationalism which once more shook, very profoundly, the unity and coherence of the Soviet bloc.

(iii) The non-ideological issues

There is no doubt that the clash of concepts, ideologies, and strategies was and remains one of the causes of the Sino–Soviet conflict. The other was and is a quite straightforward struggle for power, between the two States and the two parties as such. This is why the ideological terminology often served only to mask other equally real issues. This is also why ideological differences were muted when the two Powers and parties were able to collaborate positively and smoothly on non-ideological, economic, diplomatic or military matters (as between 1957 and 1959). Conversely it explains why, when the going became rough again, the doctrinal contradictions were exacerbated.

The seeds of this struggle for power between Communist Russia and Communist China, when it took root for good at the threshold of the fifties and thereafter, were territorial, racial, economic and technological.

(a) Territorial

Mao Tse-tung, who as recently as 1964 said in an interview given to Japanese journalists that Russia occupied too many territories which did not belong to her in Asia and in Europe, is from this point of view Sun Yat-sen's heir. Sun Yat-sen stressed in 1924 in his main work, *The Three Principles of the People*, that:

During her period of imperialism, Russia adhered to a policy of aggression and strove to expand her territory. During the past century, China had lost a vast amount of territory. At the hands of Russia, China had lost the entire territory east of the river Seleriga and Lake Baikal, including Western Transbaikalia, Eastern Transbaikalia, the Amur region, the Maritime provinces, Sakhalin and Kamchatka.

Communist China was as eager as her predecessor to ask Russia to settle all remaining territorial questions as well as the status of Outer Mongolia as a zone of influence shared between Russia and China, and to decide the reparations to be paid by Soviet Russia for the massive looting her armies had perpetrated in Manchuria at the end of the Second World War. Finally, the conflicting views of the two Powers with regard to India were to play an outstanding part in the conflict.

(b) Racial

The Russian people's atavistic fear of the enormous mass of Asiatics who, coming from unfathomable demographic reserves, press westward on the frontiers of the USSR, is a reality. The Chinese Communists are well aware of this. In an article of 21 October 1963 entitled 'Analogies of Neo-Colonialism' published by the *People's Daily* and the *Red Flag*, the leaders of the CPSU were attacked for having 'raised a hue and cry about the "yellow peril" and the imminent menace of Genghis Khan' and for wishing 'to step into the shoes of [Kaiser] Wilhelm II in propagating the theory of the yellow peril'. The fear of the 'yellow men' was aggravated in the Russian historical memory by the defeat which Tsarist Russia suffered in 1905 at the hands of the Japanese. This was described by Sun Yat-sen again in 1924, in the book already referred to, in the following words:

When as a result of the Russo-Japanese war, Japan drove Russia out of Korea and Southern Manchuria, smashed the Russian dream of world domination and maintained the integrity of Eastern Asia, a profound change took place in international life.

(c) Economic

When the Chinese Communists came to power in 1949, Stalin applied to Russia's relations with Communist China the prescription he used in relations with the Eastern European Communist States: he took for granted her dependence on Russian exports and technical aid – but made China pay high prices for Russian goods and insisted on the setting-up of mixed Sino–Soviet companies. This led by 1954 to a Chinese adverse balance of trade with Russia of some 900,000,000 dollars. When

in 1954 Khrushchev went to China on his first official visit he
apparently agreed to dissolve the Sino–Soviet mixed companies
and to introduce other improvements into the trade relations of
the two countries. Soviet exports to China were stepped up
from some 388 million dollars in 1950 to 954 million in 1959,
falling again in 1962 to 233 million. (The massive increase looked
even more striking when compared to the restricted Russian
exports to Eastern Europe between 1953 and 1956.) But at the
same time China reduced her adverse balance of trade by increasing her exports to Russia. By 1956–7 the trade balance
leaned in China's favour. These were also the years of the
second Chinese five-year plan and of the 'great leap forward'.
Unlike the first five-year plan, which was centred almost exclusively around Soviet imports, the second relied much more
on internal resources. The 'great leap forward', with its agricultural corollary the communes, was in fact also a tightening
of the belt: the accent fell on productivity and on the use of
domestic raw materials. It was a new Chinese autarchy, opposed
to Russia's vision of socialist international intervention through
COMECON.

(d) Technological

The dependence of China in the first five-year plan on Soviet
and Soviet bloc deliveries of industrial plants and machinery
and on the collaboration of Soviet experts and technicians was
as marked as her dependence on Soviet trade. The Chinese
Communists believed or pretended to believe that Soviet
Russia would make substantial sacrifices in her own economic
development so as to help China to 'equalize' their levels.
After 1955, they pressed Russia to share the production technique of the atom bomb with them. According to the Chinese,
in the agreement on new technology for national defence concluded between China and the Soviet Union in October 1957
Russia had agreed to provide China with a sample of an atomic
bomb and technical data concerning its manufacture. In this
respect the years 1956–8 were the most harmonious from the
point of view of trade relations, as they were also from the point
of view of ideological collaboration.

The autumn of 1957 remains the climax of the Sino–Soviet, or even more specifically the Khrushchev–Mao collaboration. To the agreements on economic and technological collaboration was added the Moscow declaration of the Eighty-One Communist Parties, which was the last document in which the Chinese and the Soviet points of view were substantially harmonized (in the 1960 statement the opposite points of view were only hostile bedfellows). It was a climax because it seemed to have settled the differences inherited from the past; and it preceded the abrupt fall into mutual hatred which was to follow. Mao's first ideological years had been an inconclusive wandering around the themes of 'the hundred flowers' and the respect for the national sovereignty and political integrity of all Communist countries and parties in the world. This, if anything, strengthened the trend in the Communist movement towards anti-Soviet centrifugalism. Internally, Mao considered the basic precepts of the Stalinist dictatorship of the proletariat as sufficient for any country building socialism. When, however, after the Twentieth Congress, he realized that Khrushchev's 'de-Stalinization' would profit the 'polycentric revisionists' and above all the Yugoslavs, he drew back. A recent Chinese document, 'The Origin and Development of the Differences', of 6 September 1963 states that: 'At no time and in no place did the Chinese Communist Party completely affirm the Twentieth Congress of the CPSU.' But in August 1957 the Soviet sputnik elated Mao; while the events in Poland and especially in Hungary confirmed his worst fears. He acted for the restoration of unity and discipline within the Communist bloc, 'headed by' the CPSU but with the intention that doctrinal matters should henceforth be supervised by the Chinese Communist Party. Mao went personally to Moscow on this occasion and although in later revelations he confessed to having accepted compromises at the time, he still considered the 1957 statement as a valid and basic text in so far as it established a 'general line' and an authority against polycentrism, denounced the dangers of revisionism, underplayed both 'peaceful coexistence' and 'peaceful transition' to socialism by stressing that revolutionary advances can be made also by 'non-peaceful means', and asserted that if imperialism unleashed a nuclear war it would condemn itself to destruction.

In the domestic field Mao felt even more strongly that the moment had come for China to take more than one short cut towards the leadership of the Communist movement. While with Soviet help China would 'equalize' its status as a world Power, with the 'fervour' of the 'great leap' and of the communes China could reach communism ahead of all other powers. But according to Soviet sources, in the summer of 1958 Khrushchev had already warned Mao about the wisdom of his economic and social ideologies. In January 1959 at the Twenty-First Congress he strongly defended the Russian model of collectivization, by then abandoned by the 'forward-leaping' Chinese, thus implicitly criticizing the communes. But already by the spring of 1959 Khrushchev's interest in the Yugoslavs and the progress of his policy of coexistence with the United States and the West estranged him from the Chinese. On 20 June, according to Chinese sources, he tore up the agreement on the new technology which contained the promise to help the Chinese with the atomic bomb. This was on the eve of his journey to the United States.

It was during the same six months that one must also place the alleged, and probable, attempt by the leaders of the CPSU to remove Mao and his followers from the leadership of the CPC. The man tipped by them was Marshal P'eng Teh-haui, the then Chinese Minister of Defence, whom Khrushchev had seen, ironically enough, in Tirana in May 1959. Marshal P'eng Teh-huai and his followers were purged by Mao. Once more the Russians appear to have failed to remove a rebellious leadership. Stalin had failed to overthrow Tito in 1948. Khrushchev, if he made the attempt, failed to remove Mao in 1959. This was of course a difficult undertaking, given the size and homogeneity of the CCP. But soon Khrushchev was going to fail to remove the rebellious leadership of the tiny Albanian party. This is the second story in the background of the Sino–Albanian–Soviet conflict.

(iv) Albania

Since her formation* Albania's main national instincts have
been her fears of her three neighbours: Greece, Italy and Yugoslavia. Although the peace conference of Versailles, at the end
of the First World War, had fully acknowledged the rights of
the Albanian people to be reunited within the boundaries of a
sovereign national state, Albania's independence and territorial
integrity were constantly challenged and indeed violated by
these three countries. They all claimed that part, or the whole, of
Albania belonged to themselves – while Albania claimed, on the
contrary, territories still held by them, the most important of
which is the region Kossovo-Metchifa (Kosmet), now part
of Yugoslavia. In a sense, Albania's national existence was
helped by the fact that the claims of the three larger neighbouring countries were mutually incompatible. This balance
of claims created a sort of *status quo*. But when, after the
collapse of the League of Nations and of the system of European security for which it stood, the Axis imposed its domination on the Continent, Mussolini's armies invaded Albania
on Good Friday, 1939, and occupied it until the end of the
war.†

The fact that the occupying Power during the war was a
Fascist Power gave the weak and factionalist Albanian Communist Party a new lease of life and a new *raison d'être*. It tried,
as in Yugoslavia, to take the lead in the 'patriotic war' by
organizing the partisans. But its own internal dissensions made
the task more difficult. The party was divided into at least four
groups, of which the most important, the *Puna*, was itself formed
by two heterogeneous layers. One was that of the intellectuals,
cosmopolitan and for the most part educated in French universities. They were headed by Enver Hoxha, the present leader

* She was a direct by-product of the Berlin Congress of 1878.
† For a detailed account of the Soviet–Albanian–Chinese conflict see
William E. Griffith: *Albania and the Sino–Soviet Rift* (Cambridge, Mass.,
1963), and as a comprehensive reference work on Albania, Stavro Skendi:
Albania (New York, 1957). On the war period see Julian Amery: *Sons of
the Eagle* (London, 1953).

of the party (who himself had spent a great part of his youth in French and Belgian colleges and universities), Pandi Kristo, Naku Spiro, Liri Gega and Mehmet Shehu, the present Prime Minister (who commanded a brigade in the Spanish Civil War and then, after being interned in France for some four years, escaped and joined the partisans in Tirana in 1942). The other layer consisted of the 'proletarians', headed by the tinsmith Koci Xoxe, and was more responsive to Tito's personal influence and that of the Yugoslav Communist Party. The three other main groups, situated in different parts of the country, were opposed to the *Puna* group – and the work of organization seemed almost hopeless.

In 1941 Tito sent emissaries of his own party who succeeded in forming a united Albanian Communist Party, uniting all the groups with the exception of one, and leading them into organized partisan activities, in which they were helped also by the British. By 1944 the Albanian Communists had been able to 'liquidate' the non-Communist partisans – also British-backed – and the Yugoslavs gained complete influence over them. They came to power in Albania in the same way and at the same time as the Yugoslav partisans in 1944 – and until 1948 were 'represented' at Communist meetings and conferences by the Yugoslav party.

Moreover, Albania as a Communist State was also, until 1948, under Yugoslav tutelage. Yugoslav credits in 1947 represented more than half of the national income. Common customs frontiers, mixed Yugoslav–Albanian companies, and common five-year plans spelt economic integration; while in the early Yugoslav plans for a Balkan federation, Albania was considered part and parcel of that country. The 'Kosmet' problem was thus treated by both sides, Yugoslav and Albanian, as partly irrelevant, if indeed some kind of federalization was to be reached. But it remained a deep wound in the national sensitivity of the Albanian people.

The Yugoslav's party's preference for the 'insurrectional and proletarian' Xoxe group was obvious. In 1944 a purge had already taken place in which members of the 'nationalist and intellectual' group of Hoxha were eliminated, and Hoxha himself had to indulge in self-criticism. By 1947, as Soviet–Yugoslav relations were deteriorating, Xoxe and his leading group tried desperately to 'integrate' Albania into Yugoslavia – but were opposed from within, effectively if silently, by Hoxha and his group.

The Soviet–Yugoslav open dispute in 1948 produced in Albania the short-lived victory of Xoxe and the pro-Yugoslavs. At the Eighth Plenum of the Albanian Communist Party of March 1948, Xoxe forced Hoxha to confess again and demoted his friends Maleshova, Dishnica and Shehu. Moreover, Xoxe asked to have the Soviet military advisers withdrawn and the Yugoslav and Albanian armies merged. This was too much for Stalin, who until his feud with Tito had allowed the Yugoslavs to handle Albania, but who since 1946 had begun to foster intrigues between the two parties, encouraging the Yugoslavs 'to swallow Albania' while at the same time strengthening the nationalist, anti-Yugoslav groups through Soviet economic and military aid and organization. While he failed after 1948 to raise the anti-Tito opposition in Yugoslavia, he succeeded in doing so in Albania. Hoxha took the lead and had Xoxe tried and shot in 1949, at the same time as Stalin's 'anti-Titoist' purges were raging in the rest of Eastern Europe. Also in 1949 Hoxha went to Moscow and succeeded in concluding a profitable and important trade and economic agreement.

Albania now became dependent on her economic relations with Soviet Russia and the countries of the Soviet bloc. The Albanian Communist Party also became the most fervent and genuinely sincere anti-Yugoslav party and continued to apply to its own methods of governing and 'building socialism' the most orthodox Stalinist precepts. For, apart from its popular anti-Yugoslav nationalist line, the Hoxha leadership knew that the Communists could remain in power in the restive country only by dint of using the sternest and most ruthless internal dictatorship on the Stalinist model.

After Stalin's death, things naturally had to change again, and radically. Hoxha had good reason to fear from the beginning of the new era that the new style of leadership might affect the two reasons for his previous collaboration: there might be a

rapprochement with the Yugoslavs, and the wind of liberalization might begin to blow. In both cases, as he must have seen it,
the Communist party's hold on power in Albania would be
jeopardized. His first reaction was, as early as 1954, to find a
reliable doctrinal and political ally in Mao, who in the eyes of
many Communist leaders had a better right to succeed Stalin
as the ideological head of world Communism than any of the
junior Soviet personalities – and in any case was preferable to,
and opposed to, Tito.

By the end of 1954 a long-term Sino–Albanian economic
agreement was concluded. By 1957 Chinese credits, which in
1955 had represented only 4·2 per cent of the total passive
trade balance of Albania, rose to 21 per cent. This gave rise to
some competition in 1957–9 between Soviet Russia and the
other countries of the Soviet bloc on one hand and China on
the other to assist Albania. By 1959 Communist Albania could
build on the massive loans granted to her by the Communist
countries of all denominations a more coherent economic plan
which led to the end of food rationing. At this point it is useful
to remember that 1956–9 were also the last years of the Sino–
Soviet idyll, which had been renewed once again because of the
Soviet–Yugoslav polemics after, and on the subject of, the
Hungarian revolution. It must also be remembered that the
Albanians delivered their strongest attack on the Yugoslavs
immediately after the Hungarian revolution and that Tito's
speech of 11 November 1956, which was the basis for the renewed Yugoslav criticism of the attitude of the CPSU towards
Eastern Europe, had been provoked by this very early Albanian
attack.

But by the end of 1959, after Khrushchev's visit to the USA,
Hoxha was as aware as Mao of the ultimate orientation the new
Soviet policy would take. Black clouds were falling rapidly on
Soviet–Albanian relations, ostensibly because of such incidents
as Khrushchev's promise to the Greek statesman, Sophocles
Venizelos, to look into the treatment of the Greek minority in
southern Albania; and because of the formidable political intrigues of the Russians and Yugoslavs, who attempted to overthrow Hoxha from within and to change the leadership. (Koco

Tashko and Livi Belishova were the presumed replacements –
and were afterwards purged and executed by Hoxha.) But
Hoxha came into the open against Khrushchev only after the
Chinese had opened fire in the spring of 1960 and after Khrushchev had counter-attacked with such violence at the Third
Congress of the Rumanian Workers' Party in Bucharest in June
of that year.

In the meantime, Hoxha was strengthening his own position,
based on the three trumps he held in his hands: the fact that
Albania was outside the range of the Soviet armies; the fact
that he could base his future stand against Soviet Russia on the
claim that he was, with Mao, doctrinally on the side of the
angels; and the fact that he would again be backed by his
nationalist Communist party provided he purged it of 'Soviet
agents' and provided he could survive the siege that Russia would
organize against him, by cooperating with China on the one side
and the West on the other.

The actual *dénouement* of the purge, the arrest and execution
of Koco Tashko and Livi Belishova, took place only in the late
summer of 1960, that is, after the Bucharest congress of June
1960 (from which Hoxha was absent, probably because he was
busy at home cleaning his own stables). But the case itself had
been heard before. According to an official Albanian statement,
the Soviet Embassy in Tirana tried to 'detach parts of the
leadership of the Albanian party from it'. The first Albanian
account accused these two leaders and some other and less
important members of the Albanian leadership of being Yugoslav–Greek–Albanian agents, but Hoxha has since openly
associated them with the Soviet plot against him in his party.
At the Twenty-Second Congress, Khrushchev himself described
the executed Albanians as leaders who 'took a stand for Albanian solidarity with the Soviet Union and other socialist
countries', and added that 'people who today advocate friendship with the Soviet Union are regarded by the Albanian leaders
as enemies'. But regrets in politics are not enough. On the
contrary, they only serve to emphasize defeat. Khrushchev's
sorrow over the fallen friends of the CPSU in Albania was
surprising confirmation of the fact that the CPSU had failed to

intervene successfully from within even in such a small party as the Albanian one. From then on the fight against both the Chinese and the Albanian parties could only be fought in public.

(v) China

When the fight came into the open at the end of June 1960 in Bucharest, on the occasion of the Third Congress of the Rumanian Workers' Party, the Chinese were already on the offensive. In April 1960 they had published, together with the article 'Long Live Leninism', their first complete manifesto for revolutionary fervour in a world Communist movement, threatened in their opinion by decay and compromise with the enemy. (Only a few days later the shooting down of an American U-2 plane over Soviet territory, at Sverdlovsk, confirmed their worst apprehensions – and led to Khrushchev's extraordinary determination to wreck, by his own behaviour, the Paris Summit Conference which he had so long prepared.) In June 1960, at the Pekin meeting of the World Trade Unions, the Chinese had also called for a vote on an organizational matter against the Soviet Union and had split the Communist parties taking part in the meeting into two opposed groups.

At the Bucharest Congress Khrushchev tried to obtain a snap condemnation of the Chinese, by launching accusations against them in a private meeting of the congress and by asking all the parties to make up their minds then and there.* The entire procedure was a surprise one. A Soviet document was circulated accusing the Chinese of factionalist behaviour. The exchanges between Khrushchev personally and the Chinese representative, Peng Chen, were acid on both sides, with the difference that while the Chinese never lost his calm and dignity, Khrushchev indulged in verbal violence and in general obstreperousness. The Communist parties obliged and all the Eastern European parties declared themselves against China, with the exception of the Albanians. But the majority of the

* The whole story is told with a remarkable wealth of detail and side-lights in Edward Crankshaw, *The New Cold War*, Penguin Books, 1963, which covers the phases of the conflict up to 1963.

delegations who attended the congress, and who were thus caught in Khrushchev's trap, were left with a certain sense of shock. While paying the lip-service asked from them in a way so reminiscent of the old Stalinist and Comintern days, they probably also induced the CPSU to call a proper meeting, properly prepared, to discuss the to them so important issues now thrown open. It was agreed that the conference should be held as soon as possible – after a preparatory commission had done the spade-work of comparing drafts and counter-drafts. The preparatory commission, held under Suslov's chairmanship (the other Soviet delegate was Frol Kozlov) and made up of twenty-one parties – the same parties which were called by Khrushchev before his fall for the preparatory meeting of 15 December 1964 – started its work in September and lasted for two weeks, from 11 to 25 November, when the meeting was held after the usual yearly celebrations of the November Bolshevik revolution.

The meeting was known as the Eighty-One Communist Parties Meeting and issued its final declaration, known by the same name, on 6 December 1960. This is one of the most inconclusive documents in the history of communism. The main issue for the solution of which the meeting had been called and around which the discussion was centred, that of 'fractionalism within the Communist movement' (by which is meant the forming by at least two parties of an opposition 'fraction'), was not even mentioned. For the Russians, who hoped above all to obtain from the conference a clear condemnation of 'fractionalism' in order to prevent the Chinese from forming opposition groups within the movement and within each Communist party, the fact that in the end nothing was said on the subject was a major defeat.

But otherwise both the meeting and the declaration worked out satisfactorily for them. At the meeting the majority of the parties openly condemned the behaviour of the Chinese party. The Chinese themselves recognized afterwards that they had been defeated in their attempt to have the Twentieth Congress of the CPSU and its main theme, de-Stalinization, corrected by the Eighty-One Parties. The rest of the points, from peaceful coexistence to revisionism, were so treated in the document that each of the two groups could afterwards quote different paragraphs from it, arguing that these endorsed their attitude. It was in fact a document showing the profound division created within the Communist movement. In the words of the Chinese assessment of the meeting, made in a summary of 6 September 1963: 'The struggle between the two lines in the international Communist movement dominated the 1960 Moscow meeting from beginning to end.' In the words of the CPSU: 'The CPC leaders were only manoeuvring when they affixed their signatures to the statement of 1960.' Both were right.

But the CPSU soon realized that if the Communist movement was left in a state of divided leadership, as reflected in the extraordinary ambivalence of the 'basic declaration of 1960', their authority would be in more serious jeopardy, for the Chinese would profit from the occasion to form in the disintegrating body more hard nuclei of their own 'fractions'. The CPSU had somehow to regain the initiative on the double front: to project for the entire Communist movement the new avenues through which the CPSU would lead it to the final victory of communism in history, and to crush the internal opposition in the bloc.

For this purpose the CPSU undertook to change its programme (the last one was still that of 1919, drafted by Lenin and adopted in the early days of the revolution). For Stalin, who concentrated exclusively, but successfully, on the realities of his rule, Lenin's programme for Utopia was good enough and could remain unchanged, as a sentimental relic. But the new leadership of the CPSU, preoccupied by the adjustment of an obsolete doctrine to the changed world and challenged from within by parties maintaining that they had more 'fervour' than the adipose CPSU, wanted to have a programme through which its voice could be heard anew in the new world of the mid twentieth century. For the purpose of winning popularity in Africa and Asia the 'programme' adopted in 1961 had obvious advantages. 'It has a strong element of moral fervour. It embraces in one grand sweep two events as part of one and the same historical process: the progressive development of the

USSR since 1917 and the progressive collapse of colonialism. It offers a confident prediction of Soviet progress in the immediate and determined future – in the next twenty years.'* The Chinese comment in the document of 6 September 1963, previously quoted, was that it 'is a revisionist programme for the preservation or restoration of capitalism'.

But, after all, the big battle of the Twenty-Second Congress was not fought over the irrelevant programme. How irrelevant it was was shown by the short time ultimately given at the congress to its discussion: the last two days out of two weeks. The main battle was fought on the problem of de-Stalinization, with its two dramatic corollaries: the elimination of Stalin's corpse from the Mausoleum, and the elimination of the Stalinist Albanians from the Communist movement. For both operations, Khrushchev provided the atmosphere of drama and suspense which was one of his greatest assets as a politician. Concentrating on the dead Stalin, not only on his memory but on his actual preserved corpse, Khrushchev was really performing, without knowing it, the primitive rite described by anthropologists as 'the expulsion of embodied evils' (and which in Frazer's *Golden Bough* is included in the chapter of 'Public Scapegoats'). For Khrushchev, as for the priests and sorcerers of the primitive tribes, what counted was the effect of the ritual on the community; the greater its horror, the more salutary its effects. The fact itself of the exhumation and degradation was heady stuff. But some details were even more inebriating, such as the confession made by an old woman delegate, Lazurkina, that Lenin appeared in her dreams to complain that he was forced to share a tomb with Stalin. In the end the macabre deed was carried out in an atmosphere of electric excitement and shattering emotion. Everyone knew that the expulsion of the corpse was in fact the ritual for the expulsion of the anti-party opposition, of Mao and of the Albanians.

As for the Albanians – they were simply not invited (nor were the Yugoslavs, but for different reasons). This had been a decision solely of the hosts. Symbolically it amounted to the

* Leonard Schapiro, in his introduction to *The USSR and the Future, an Analysis of the New Programme of the CPSU* (London, 1963).

elimination of the Albanians by the leading party of the movement. In the same symbolic way it amounted to the end of the
'fraction' in the movement, for only the Albanians had supported the Chinese in Bucharest in 1960. Khrushchev explained
this implicit elimination by the assertion that the Albanians had
defied the 1957 and 1960 rules of discipline and inter-party
behaviour, and after fruitless attempts to restore Soviet–
Albanian friendship and the working of inter-bloc discipline,
the Soviet leadership had been convinced that the Albanians
had placed themselves outside the Communist family, whose
'internationalist duty' it was now to acknowledge this fact
publicly. The Chinese, taken by surprise by the violence of both
moves, against Stalin and against the Albanians, reacted at
once. In his reply Chou En-lai spoke of the 'socialist camp
comprising twelve fraternal countries from the Korean Democratic Republic to the Albanian People's Republic'. This echoed
the theme of 'objective membership', as in the affairs of the
Communist world. Then he left the congress precipitately – but
not without finding time to lay a wreath on Stalin's new and
humble grave. Later still, the Chinese stated that: 'The Twenty-
Second Congress of the CPSU in October 1961 marked a new
low in the leadership of the CPSU's efforts to oppose Marxism–
Leninism and split the socialist camp and the international
Communist movement.'

This was not far from the truth. Inside the movement, inside
the Communist camp of ruling parties and even in the Soviet
bloc, the fact that Albania and her party, anathematized by the
CPSU and by the Soviet Union, later defied them successfully
and indeed violently led to a permanent split and sank Soviet
Russia's international authority to a yet lower level. It also gave
to all the Communist parties, and notably within the Soviet
bloc to the oppressed but restive Rumanian Workers' Party, the
assurance that even with a less felicitous geo-political situation
than that of Albania, Rumania too could find its escape through
the 'dogmatist anti-Soviet' triangular solution.

Outside the movement the split was to emerge later on quite a
different plane: that of world events. The two camps, led by two
parties, were soon to find themselves opposed on two issues of

supreme importance for the peace of the entire world: the handling of the Cuban crisis by Soviet Russia, and the handling of the war with India by Communist China. Here the ideological themes of 'peaceful coexistence' and of 'justified wars' were going to be heard amidst the din of rapid preparations for what could have been the beginning of the Third World War.

(vi) Khrushchev, Cuba and China

Even during his ten crowded years of leadership and even more so after his fall in October 1964, Khrushchev made one wonder whether his ebullience, which almost amounted to frenzy, was generated by a visceral optimism or whether it was assumed and hid a lucid, even melancholy, assessment of the shrinking limits of Russian communism in the world and in history. How much in him was primeval force, an instinctive aggressiveness and drive, and how much was a conscious effort to inspire and animate a declining organism? The answer probably lies somewhere in the middle. His natural vitality and robustness surely helped to carry with them not only his listeners and followers but himself too. But on the other hand he was not stupid, and he was one of the few men in the world who fully realized how locked in its own contradictions and difficulties Soviet Russia had come to be of late.

He knew that her economic advance would be for ever mortgaged by her agriculture, which he had tried to boost by mechanization, the opening of virgin lands and better agrotechnical methods, but to no avail so long as it remained imprisoned within the Communist dogma of collectivization. He knew that without a fast economic advance Russia could not lead the world in her standard of living, could not even catch up with the Western levels or continue her own efforts at the pace which he imposed between 1955 and 1961. He knew that the new health and progress of the free world meant the dwindling of the chances of Communist advance, either by the revolution of the 'discontented masses' or by Stalin's method of revolution by military intervention. He knew that revolutionary stagnation brought with it revolutionary disintegration

– the first effects of which Stalin and he had already experienced. He knew that while the Communist camp showed signs of increased centrifugalism, in the capitalist West there had been in the fifties a surprising effort towards coordination and even integration. He knew, finally, that as long as the German problem was not solved in Russia's favour, not only would there be no further opening for her advance, but it would prove very hard to hold Eastern Germany – and Eastern Europe. Twice during his rule he had given the West an ultimatum on the Berlin question and twice he had had to call it off; and he had been forced at last in desperation to build the Berlin Wall, the ugliest symbol of Communist impotence.

Yet it was in the political field that some moves could still be tried in the otherwise immobile perspective. For undertaking the Cuban adventure of October 1962 first the Chinese and later his successors in the leadership of the CPSU criticized him for having done both too much and too little – for aggression and capitulation. But this was probably a desperate Soviet attempt to circumvent the obvious superiority of the USA in nuclear weapons, the means of launching them and the deployment of missile bases.

This superiority was the ultimate reason why Khrushchev, unlike Mao, knew that he could not take the risk of trying to conquer new positions which the West or the USA might defend with all their means. The mounting of Russian missile bases in Cuba would affect American policy in the event of another showdown on Berlin and could, presumably, change the entire outlook for Russia. If this was one of the most important reasons which explain Khrushchev's gamble in Cuba (otherwise there are few reasons for which he could have indulged in such a venture), then, too, he must also have realized that, if caught in the exercise, he would have to retreat. He did so, after seven days of crisis, when he was convinced that President Kennedy meant what he had said – and he left on a hardly consoling compromise that the USA would, in its turn, not invade Cuba once the Soviet military had left it. Kennedy was violently criticized in his country by the right-wing opposition and never forgiven for having made this concession. Yet for the

contemporary historian Cuba did represent a great watershed
in East–West relations. The fact that the USA had shown that
in some cases aggression could bring disaster to the aggressor,
and perhaps to large parts of the world too, taught the more
reasonable Communists a supplementary lesson of wisdom.
From Cuba onwards the way to better US–USSR relations
was opened; and the nuclear test ban treaty was signed less
than a year later.

But Khrushchev was far more violently criticized than
Kennedy. The episode brought the Chinese, the North Korean
and the Albanian parties to a state of paroxysm. 'Capitulation-
ism' and 'Munich' were the most frequently heard epithets.
The Chinese especially saw in this the dramatic epitome of the
entire liquidationist Khrushchevian policy throughout the world
and on all fronts of the world revolution. This was the proof for
them that the Soviet nuclear weapon would only be used to
further Russia's policy as a Great Power and not as a revolutionary leader. In an official Chinese statement of 18 November
1963 it was stated that:

> The fact is that when the leaders of the CPSU brandish their
> nuclear weapons it is not really to support the people's anti-
> imperialist struggles . . . During the Caribbean crisis, for instance,
> they engaged in speculative opportunistic and irresponsible nuclear
> gambling for *ulterior motives*. As soon as their *nuclear blackmail* is
> seen through and is countered in kind, they retreat one step after
> another, and lose all by their nuclear gambling [my italics].

Moreover, the Chinese added fuel to the fire by their own war
with India during the Cuban crisis. The first serious border
incident between China and India occurred in September 1959.
Ever since, the leadership of the CPSU has adopted an attitude
of neutrality towards Chinese claims against India. This was one
of the first causes of the Sino–Soviet estrangement, and perhaps
also one of the secondary reasons why the USSR in 1959 tore
up its commitment to help China to build the atom bomb. On 20
October 1962, just five days before the Cuban crisis, the
Chinese armies attacked, passing into Indian territory at the
north-east frontier area and in Ladakh. When Khrushchev had

already promised to withdraw the Soviet military and bases from Cuba, the Chinese armies were triumphantly driving back the poorly prepared Indian forces. By the end of November they had achieved their announced objective – the re-occupation of Ladakh – and they then proudly and unilaterally withdrew from the other theatres of operation which they had opened. This was deliberately done to contrast with Russia's precipitate and incoherent withdrawal from Cuba. But the leaders of the USSR found in turn a good opportunity to criticize the Chinese. In the statement of the Soviet Government of 21 September 1963 the Chinese were reminded that already in 1959 the Soviet leaders had told them that the aggravation of the dispute over frontier territories in the Himalayas was fraught with negative consequences:

Everyone can now see that the Chinese–Indian conflict in the Himalayas had the most negative consequences for the cause of peace; inflicted great harm on the unity of the anti-imperialist front in Asia . . . and China's prestige in the eyes of the peoples of the world, and especially of the Afro-Asian peoples, had certainly not grown.

This criticism, too, was in great measure justified.

Thus, with their external adventures concluded in a very controversial way, the two Communist Powers fell back into their own open polemics, after having stabbed each other in the back in moments of supreme importance. In a series of four Communist Party Congresses held in less than two months at the end of 1962, namely those of the Bulgarian, Hungarian, Czechoslovak and Italian Communist Parties, the Soviet Union and China used the rostrums for mutual vilification. The CPSU used the gatherings to provoke as far and as often as possible declarations of loyalty towards itself by the various Communist Parties. Their leadership was courted and pressed from both sides; in many of them lines of cleavage were already appearing, as some non-ruling parties began to split into pro-Russian and pro-Chinese wings.

The East European parties, with the exception of the Albanians, were obviously all leaning towards Khrushchev's policy of 'peaceful coexistence'. When the climax of his polemic with the Chinese on this particular point came, after the signing of the partial nuclear test ban treaty on 25 July 1963, they all backed Soviet Russia sincerely against China and criticized the Chinese views on the matter. But they were less eager, all of them, to encourage Khrushchev in his other major plan: that of a great showdown with China, with the ultimate possibility of the excommunication of the CCP; and some of them were resolutely opposed to such an idea even for ideological reasons.

But with this we come to another development, perhaps at first sight of minor importance, but in fact deeply significant, which added to Khrushchev's troubles. It led him and the CPSU into further defeat; disturbed considerably the waters of the Soviet bloc; complicated all the issues by yet another internal dissension and polemic; and altogether helped towards the crystallization of a more neutral and, indeed, detached attitude on the part of the Eastern European parties towards the CPSU. This was Khrushchev's effort during 1962–3 to integrate Eastern Europe economically under the aegis of COMECON, which failed because of the Rumanian Workers' Party's opposition to it.

4 The Neutralists (1963 onwards)

The range of events surveyed from now on defeat by their nearness in time not only historians but also the political analysts rash enough to make the attempt to place them in a proper perspective. It is impossible at this stage to assess clearly the causes and the effects of Khrushchev's fall and of its impact on the future development of Sino–Soviet relations. Much more dust will have to settle before the final contours emerge.

It so happens, however, that, as far as the relations between Soviet Russia and the Eastern European countries are concerned, the main trends described in earlier chapters continued and indeed were strengthened by the major developments with which these last pages will deal. The rebellion of the Rumanian Workers' Party against Khrushchev's plans for the further economic integration of the Soviet bloc was yet another defeat for the CPSU, its prestige and its authority. The specific attitude taken by the Rumanians in the dispute struck, however, a different note and went much farther than the economic issue would have warranted by itself. It was a blend of nationalism, of ideological nonconformism, and of political opportunism, which together led to a general aloofness amounting to neutralism.

Moreover, Khrushchev, caught in mounting competition with the Chinese, and pressing for the summoning of a conference in which the Communist world-movement would be called upon to decide between the two opposite points of view, must have seen with some surprise that many Eastern European and European parties, his natural allies in the 'revisionist' line for which the Chinese were attacking him, showed in this burning issue the same uneasy detachment.

The father of Communist polycentrism, Togliatti, died in 1964 in Soviet Russia. His political testament, recommending still greater caution in the handling of this major question and at the same time warning the smaller parties against the dangers of the re-establishment of a general party line controlled from one centre, amounted in fact to a new formulation of this intra-bloc neutralism. Khrushchev's fall was influenced by the fact that he failed to get a warm response from the Soviet bloc and the European and Western parties when in the preparatory stages of the ultimate showdown with the CPC he sounded his last clarion call to rally around the CPSU. The anxiety shown by both Western and Eastern European parties about the nature of his overthrow and the consequences of his fall were accompanied by an increased awareness of the advantages of the loosening of their former tight disciplinary ties with the CPSU which they had recently obtained. Former projects of bringing closer together parties and countries which by their size, their geo-political conditions and their ideological positions found them-selves situated between Great Powers in conflict became topical once more and acquired new energy. These trends were not and could not be reversed. But when events are too close to be analysed one can only speculate about the future.

(i) The Rumanians versus COMECON

The triangular conflict between the Rumanian Workers' Party, the Council for Mutual Economic Assistance and Khrushchev as leader of the CPSU and of the Soviet Union became public only in the summer of 1962. Up till then two contrary trends had appeared within the commonwealth of Communist coun-tries, which from a political point of view form the Warsaw Pact bloc and from an economic point of view, COMECON.

On the one hand, there was the new trend shown by the leadership of the Rumanian Workers' Party with its own new economic policy of speedy and autarchic 'many-sided' in-dustrialization, as formulated since 1958 and embodied in the Third Economic Plan of 1960.

On the other, there was the new school of thought among the other leading Communist Parties – the Czechoslovak, the East German, and to some extent the Polish and Hungarian as well, backed afterwards by the Soviet Union itself – which proclaimed that in the new circumstances created by the policy of peaceful coexistence – and especially by the emergence of the European Common Market – the socialist countries should proceed with a proper regional economic integration in order to attain national and regional efficiency.

The case of Rumania cannot be understood without taking into consideration above all her backwardness and her sense of inferiority arising from her economic position within the bloc. Even before the war, Rumania – one of the richest, if not the richest in raw materials and natural resources of all the Eastern European countries – was much less developed than, for instance, Czechoslovakia, and indeed her indices of *per capita* industrial production and national income were among the lowest, and her agricultural overpopulation – a classical sign of economic maladjustment – was among the highest.

With the coming of the Communists to power in Eastern Europe, this time-lag was aggravated. When, during the open Rumanian–COMECON quarrel, statistics were hurled from one side to the other, the image projected by the East German or Czechoslovak statistics (but not the Rumanian) was that while Rumania for instance in 1960 still had only one worker per 8·3 per cent inhabitants, East Germany had 1 worker per 2·8 per cent, the USSR 1 per 4·4 per cent and Poland 1 per 4·1 per cent. Industrial production in Rumania was 36 in 1960 as compared to 100 for East Germany and 110 for Czechoslovakia.

The report presented by Gheorghiu-Dej at an enlarged Central Committee Plenary meeting in November 1958 was boastful. It forecast an era of rapid industrialization and of total collectivization (formulae which had been dropped during the five years of the new course and of the Polish and Hungarian events). All this was later embodied in the Third Economic Plan, presented at the Third Congress in 1960. The targets set were the highest, not only for Rumania, but for the whole of Eastern Europe, both for rate of growth of industrial production and capital investment; and the entire scheme of the plan was based on the idea of the multilateral development of all branches of industry based on the creation in Rumania of a vaster and self-contained machine-building and iron and steel industry. Specifically, the plan announced that an entirely new plant was to be erected in Galati, which by 1970, when it was due to start production, would add another four million tons a year to the three million produced by the older plants, thus bringing the whole production to seven million tons a year, more than the 1962 production of either Poland, Eastern Germany or Czechoslovakia.

The trends in the rest of the Soviet bloc ran in the opposite direction. There was, of course, the Sino–Soviet schism, but there was also something else. The economic integration of Western Europe in 1960–2 was really gathering momentum, surprising everyone, but leaving the Marxist economists at a loss for an explanation. Proud parties, such as the Polish one, jealous of their national independence within the bloc, thought that closer COMECON cooperation and coordination, which was being openly advocated, might be the answer. Specialization for greater efficiency was the current slogan. Draft plans for such specialization were being circulated. Within such a framework, the new Rumanian plan stood out like a sore thumb.

At the beginning of 1962, the Polish Communist Party took the initiative of calling a special session of the COMECON council to be attended by all first secretaries. It was held in June in Moscow, and produced two main results. In the first place COMECON was endowed with a new organ, an executive committee which was situated between the council itself, which met too rarely, and the nineteen standing commissions which now existed. The executive committee, which was to meet regularly, could take decisions on organizational matters. But even the new organ was, as it still is, an international body and not a supra-national one, and the rule as set out in the charter of COMECON is that all decisions should be taken with the unanimous approval of all member states, which is tantamount to saying that each member has a full veto. The second result of the June meeting was the publication of a vast and vague document called *The Basic Principles of the International*

Socialist Division of Labour. Like the 1960 Moscow declaration of the Eighty-One Communist Parties, the 17 June 1962 COMECON Principles comprises only a patchwork of contradictory statements put together so as to allow each party to quote passages confirming its own point of view.

Within COMECON there were three schools of thought on the subject of economic integration. The first was the Russian. The Russian doctrine recognized that there are for the time being, and there will probably be so long as frontiers continue to exist, three categories of economic States. The first is the Great Power, which alone can have a universal industrialization and one which cannot be equalled by the smaller countries. Then there are the countries which, because of their past capitalist industrialization, play in the new economic family and in its subsequent specialization the natural part of the industrial partners and producers. And then there are the agrarian-industrial and industrial-agrarian countries. These countries will not only progress, but will be helped by the entire family to progress and to raise their economic level. But they cannot do this by clinging to their old parochial claims to achieve complete or 'universal' industrialization. They must specialize and their specialization must start from their present structure. This is where the problem of rhythm is important. One of the Rumanian arguments in the first phase of the quarrel with COMECON illustrates this problem. The Rumanians argued that integration within COMECON should start later, after the Rumanian economy had transformed its economic structure; it would thus align itself with COMECON only after it had attained a higher economic status. This reasoning lies behind the insistence of all the less-developed Communist countries from China to Rumania on speedy industrialization in order to catch up in the shortest possible time with the more developed countries.

The second school of thought was bluntly put and then withdrawn by the East Germans. The East German economists grouped around the review *Wirtschafts–Wissenschaft* published an article in the April 1963 issue by Dr Huber, a well-known East German economist, entitled 'The Determination of the

Level of Economic Development of a Socialist Country'. Huber's first point was that in order to measure the level one has to find the proper yardstick. That yardstick is labour productivity and it is formed by the indices of national income, of total industrial production, of comparative industrial agricultural output and of the rate of growth of industrial production. He showed that in the case of Rumania the growth of industrial production did not always bring about a growth of national productivity and therefore of the level of productivity. He went on to ask why in the socialist international division of labour small countries should not follow the example of some small capitalist countries, especially the Netherlands and Denmark, where general productivity is very high although industrialization is circumscribed. He proposed that small socialist countries should follow what he defined as passive industrialization and should attune their plans and aims in this realistic way. (When after the First Secretaries' meeting of July 1963 the entire matter was officially dropped, the editorial board of *Wirtschafts–Wissenschaft* condemned Huber's theses in a special statement, stating that his views were un-Marxist and apologizing for having published the article.)

The third school of thought is the Rumanian. The best statement of its views is a study in the monthly *Probleme Economice* of July 1963 entitled 'The Importance of the Rhythms of Development for the Equalization of the Economic Levels of the Socialist Countries'. The study states that it is inconceivable that communism can be built in the world while the differences between developed and undeveloped countries were maintained. The only way to abolish these differences is by accelerating the rhythm of development of the many-sided industries based on the national heavy industry. The study goes on to attack the criterion of efficiency, which was Khrushchev's main slogan: 'At certain times and in certain places situations may prevail in the light of which economic or even social-political considerations should be put first, while on the contrary the exclusive pursuit of efficiency should naturally be relegated to the secondary plane.' With this the wheel had come full circle. The economic doctrine of the Rumanians was brought back to the plane of political considerations and of national passions.

But in the meantime this deep ideological conflict had been transformed into a real drama by the fact that Khrushchev, as leader of the CPSU and of the USSR, which until now had watched the discussion 'impartially', spoke out, under pressure from the East German, the Czechoslovak and the Polish parties, and gave his final views on the subject.

In September 1962, Khrushchev published a long article entitled 'Vital Questions of the Development of the Socialist World System in Problems of Peace and Socialism', and on 19 November 1962 in his report to the Central Committee of the CPSU he completed it by making practical proposals. In his article he began by quoting Lenin who, he said, had foreseen the collaboration of socialist nations as taking place in a single world-wide cooperation. He said that it had taken thirty years for Lenin's ideal to come true, with the foundation in 1949 of COMECON. He recognized that for a few years COMECON had only been a solid basis for increasing trade and collaboration between member states. He also recognized that what made further integration more difficult was the fact that some of the countries of the bloc were less developed than others. Moreover, he added, 'The fact that these countries had been at some time part of the capitalist world system had left them with an economically unjustified universalization of industry based on small-quantity production.' He went on to say that this kind of universalization had to be brought to an end because small countries cannot produce everything. This was permissible only 'to the big Powers, for they can afford to have a more universal industry, thanks to specialization and coordination within their countries and to a relatively big home market'. In a veiled reference to Rumania he referred to socialist countries which in order to provide themselves with everything 'purchased goods on the side', that is in markets other than COMECON; and indeed the Rumanians were making great progress in their trade with the West. Therefore, concluded Khrushchev, the time had come to proceed with a more radical integration. All the countries concerned were ripe enough. What was needed was a common will and a common organ for making decisions. In his speech to the November Plenum, one of his main proposals was the creation of a supra-national organ, some kind of independent planning body which could issue instructions and orders to all the members of COMECON.

Two days after Khrushchev spoke in Moscow, on 21 November 1962, the Rumanian Central Committee met and acknowledged in a communiqué that for two days it had discussed the problem of relations between Rumania and the other COMECON countries. It seems to have been at this meeting that the leadership of the Rumanian Workers' Party realized that it was useless to continue to hide the truth from the rank and file and leave them, as before, under the impression that Soviet Russia supported the Rumanian point of view.

The meeting of the executive committee of COMECON in February 1963 can be taken as the point of no return in the dispute. It was then that the Rumanians received the list of demands which were made on them in view of the future 'international socialist division of labour'. The demands, from what is known of them, were unjust. Rumania was asked to make sacrifices without equal compensation. She was asked to tone down and to alter substantially her own industrialization plans so as not to duplicate industries which flourished in Czechoslovakia and East Germany and to avoid competing with their exports in the protected market of the Soviet bloc. Such demands would have affected the whole economic future of the country and destroyed its last chance of reaching a higher stage of economic development. Finally, Rumania was asked to agree in advance to share in plans to 'divide the region into economic sub-units' which ran contrary not only to her national economic interests but even to her overall national interests.

These plans seem to have borne a close resemblance to the theses of a study published in the autumn of 1964 in the *Moscow University Herald* by Professor I. B. Valev of Moscow University. Valev showed that there should be an economic unit called the Danubian Complex whereby Rumania as an economic

F

unit could be halved, Transylvania and Moldavia being integrated with Hungary and Czechoslovakia, leaving the southern
part of Rumania with Bulgaria and part of the Ukraine as a
'south-eastern unit'. He was attacked in the Rumanian *Viata
Economica* of July 1964, which said that 'such plans disregard
Rumania's sovereignty and propose to dismember her territory
and national economy'.

The Rumanian refusal at the February COMECON meeting was absolute. Even the danger of being eliminated from
COMECON altogether obviously left her unmoved. On 5
March the Rumanian Central Committee met again and held a
four-day meeting on COMECON issues, at the end of which
they stated that the entire Central Committee approved of all
that the Rumanian representative had said in the COMECON
meeting and confirmed that he had only carried out his instructions. The communiqué went on to state that the collaboration
with COMECON was understood to be very useful but only
as a means of coordination (and not of integration). This coordination could be attained by means of bilateral (and not
multilateral) negotiations between member states and in any
case only on the basis of the full equality of rights of all the
sovereign countries. These became and have remained the main
tenets of the Rumanians in this dispute. Moreover, once
expressed in the March 1963 communiqué, they were afterwards
fed ideologically to all layers of the party and all strata of the
population. Meetings were held throughout the country. A
letter from the party was circulated stating that in spite of the
basic friendship between the RPR and the USSR, on this
issue the parties could only differ.

Like all parties which had found themselves in conflict with
the views of the Russians, the Rumanian Workers' Party
decided to take into its confidence sectors of the party and of
society as broad as possible. Like Gomulka in Poland in 1956
and Hoxha in Albania in 1960 they knew that the national feel-
ings of the people and also their anti-Soviet sentiments would
outweigh the antipathy which they themselves inspired. They
relied on the idea of national pride and reaped a useful harvest.

Like Hoxha in Albania, they were able to consolidate their own political and ideological positions. The leadership of the Rumanian Workers' Party, which had been one of the most reluctant to de-Stalinize, decided to continue on the basis of the old formula of the dictatorship of the proletariat: the industrialization, collectivization and maintenance of the coercive state and its functions. In the heat of the economic argument with COMECON they crystallized this into a doctrine of their own – a sort of dynamic national dogmatism. While on matters of general foreign policy, peaceful coexistence and nuclear disarmament the Rumanian party followed the Moscow line, on matters of inter-party relations and of Communist political philosophy they were much closer to the dogmatist point of view. They tried to reach, and succeeded in reaching, a quasi-neutral position which was not only to their advantage within the bloc and COMECON but also improved considerably their political and economic relations with the West.

Having thus consolidated their own position at home, the Rumanian Workers' Party prepared for the next steps. One problem still looming on the horizon was the coming meeting of the First Secretaries to discuss the Khrushchev proposal for a supra-national planning body and the Rumanian refusal. The meeting was held in July 1963. But before it was held the Rumanian Workers' Party received important help from three different sources. From the West it received welcome economic and financial help and the assurance that the goods needed for Rumanian industrialization could be purchased more cheaply from various Western countries and would be of better quality. The Rumanian trade delegations showed initiative in these matters, as for instance in the case of their economic relations with West Germany, which has now become one of their major trading partners and with which, after Poland, the Rumanians were the first to re-establish diplomatic trade relations. But the Rumanians were the first Communist country to recognize in a trade agreement that for trade and economic purposes West Berlin should be considered as an integral part of the Federal German Republic. The Hungarians followed suit a few days later, but the precedent, much to Ulbricht's distaste, had already been established by the Rumanians.

The Chinese also gave massive help to the Rumanians. When in June 1963 the Chinese published for the first time the twenty-five points which according to them contained the basic differences between their own ideology and that of the Russians, the CPSU demanded that all the Eastern Europeans should ignore it. This instruction was obeyed in all the people's democracies with the exceptions of Albania and Rumania. The Rumanians published the full text on 20 June. One of the twenty-five points put forward by the Chinese was of vital importance for the Rumanians:

> It is absolutely necessary for socialist countries to practise mutual economic assistance, cooperation and exchange. Such economic co-operation must be based on the principles of complete equality, mutual benefit and comradely mutual assistance. It would be great-power chauvinism to deny these principles and in the name of the international division of labour and specialization to impose one's will on others, to infringe or harm the interests of their people.

This was also a clear warning to Khrushchev that if Rumania was going to be eliminated from the 'COMECON family' the Chinese and Albanian parties would find new grounds for their denunciations of Soviet Russia.

And thirdly help came to Rumania from yet another quarter: from Mao Tse-tung's arch-enemy, Tito. On 12 June 1963 the Rumanians announced the conclusion of an agreement with Yugoslavia for the construction of the greatest hydro-electric power station ever to be built in Europe, to cost some hundred and fifty million pounds and to be built and financed by the two countries alone. This was another Rumanian blow to COMECON. For at the moment when she was obstructing all the efforts to coordinate plans within its orbit and refusing to take a greater part in the investment pool schemes, to announce in the same breath such a vast programme of invest-ment and collaboration with a non-COMECON country was not simply an act of defiance. It was the finalization of the divorce.

Supported thus from the right and from the left, Gheorghiu-
Dej, who was not present at the Communist summit meeting in
East Berlin on the occasion of Ulbricht's seventieth birthday,
attended the First Secretaries' meeting in Moscow at the end of
July. The debate on the decision to transform COMECON
into a supra-national authority led to a foregone conclusion.
As usual there were two meetings, one of the Warsaw Pact and
one of COMECON. At the Warsaw Pact meeting Gheorghiu-
Dej supported the policy of peaceful coexistence and approved
vehemently of the recently signed Soviet–American agreement
on the cessation of nuclear tests, which the Chinese had denounced with great violence. But at the COMECON meeting
he was the same defiant and adamant opponent – and with so
much success that in the final communiqué published on 27
July all the Rumanian formulae – coordination, bilateralism,
full sovereignty – were to be found and nowhere was Khrushchev's supra-national organ even mentioned or implied.
COMECON remained a consultative body and as such
crippled and impotent. The Rumanian plans were pursued with
renewed enthusiasm. Khrushchev and the CPSU suffered a
stinging defeat of prestige and authority.

(ii) Towards a European 'Communist neutralism'?

The Rumanian breakthrough was a direct consequence of the
breaches already made in the formerly united Communist
movement. It was encouraged by the revisionists' reaction
against Stalin's exploitation and oppression. It was also an
immediate result of the successful Albanian defiance, which
was itself the first European reverberation of the Chinese
extra-continental opposition to Khrushchev's policies of de-
Stalinization. Without these precedents, the benefits of which
it inherited, the Rumanian stand would have been inconceivable.

But once achieved it showed a specific character of its own
which afterwards influenced some developments and added its
own impetus to the process of disintegration which had already
set in. This was the first time that a party within the Soviet bloc

had succeeded in adopting in some respects a neutral line, and it is probable that the Rumanian defiance played a part in precipitating Khrushchev's fall.

The expression 'Communist neutralism' has been applied until now in Communist terminology to the attitude of the four Communist parties which, at the beginning of the Sino–Soviet conflict in 1960, refused to take sides on the various issues for which the two super-party rivals were proposing alternative solutions; they were the Cuban party and the three Asian parties, of North Korea, North Vietnam and Indonesia. The three Asian parties have since made up their minds and are now standing firmly on China's side.

The Rumanian Communist neutral line also emerged, to begin with, in the troubled realm of ideology. The first public signs of the aloofness of the Rumanian Workers' Party towards the Sino–Soviet dispute were to be found in the scrupulous insistence with which since 1962 it has published the texts of both parties – Soviet and Chinese together – while the media of information of the Soviet bloc carried only the Soviet texts. Moreover, ever since the Twenty-Second Congress of the CPSU the Rumanian Workers' Party had evaded producing a full and unreserved endorsement of Soviet criticism of the Chinese. While the other Soviet bloc parties did so frequently and added their own heat to the polemic, the Rumanian Workers' Party said as little as possible and kept as closely as it could to general formulae. This was not only a matter of style: even when the controversy with Khrushchev and COMECON reached its peak the Rumanian Workers' Party behaved with a characteristically Byzantine composure and sense of ceremony. But its attitude towards the deeper ideological issues was in fact ambivalent. It shared with Albania and China the belief that without the full maintenance of the Leninist–Stalinist dictatorship of the proletariat there would be no future for the Communist States; but it also fully accepted the Soviet Union's foreign policy of peaceful coexistence and cooperation with the West, with the proviso that Rumania itself should reap the benefits of such a policy. The fundamental contradiction between these ideological positions was veiled by the Rumanian

Communists with the argument of the primacy of the national interests.

Indeed, the Rumanian Workers' Party expressed its new-found self-confidence, after the victory against COMECON of July 1963, by making a public show of the new nationalistic and specifically anti-Russian spirit by which it was animated. It achieved by this two things: it was able to reverse the entire trend of almost twenty years of compulsory Russianization; and it also was able to play to the gallery of the Rumanian people. The national 'decompression' was rapidly and successfully effected. Starting from the summer of 1963 the measures of de-Russianization exploded in public. In the previous years some steps had quietly been taken. Most urgent and effective are the purges of Moscow-trained personnel from the party and security cadres, and since 1962 the intensive education of the rank and file and of all layers of the population on the Rumanian stand against the USSR.

There had also been a noticeable tendency to restore Rumanian culture and tradition to the place of honour. But from the summer of 1963 both trends gathered speed. The Russian bookshop and the Russian institute were closed. Most of the streets of Bucharest and of other cities which had been given Russian names reverted to their old Rumanian names. Classical Rumanian works, such as Iorga's history of Rumania, banished since the Communists came to power, and contemporary writings, such as Eugène Ionesco's plays, reappeared or appeared for the first time in public.

The criticism of Khrushchev soon turned to general contempt of all things Russian. Rumania is now the country in the Soviet bloc in which anti-Russian feeling is most openly expressed – and where in official quarters a new national fervour seems to be the answer to all questions, ideological or political, which the Rumanian people might ask in connexion with the mainten-ance of the old Stalinist way of ruling the country. The anti-Soviet feeling, skilfully played up, carried the sympathy of the people.

From the summer of 1963, the Rumanian Workers' Party

abandoned its previously diffident attitude towards taking sides in the ideological conflict, and began to assert itself actively as a mediator. The first significant outward sign of this new departure was an article published by the Rumanian Prime Minister, Ion Gheorghe Maurer, in *The World Marxist Review* of September 1963, on the occasion of the anniversary of the Moscow declaration of the Eighty-One Communist Parties of October 1960. One of the main themes of the article was that, whatever the differences of views between brotherly parties, it was inconceivable that they should be aired in hostile and sterile polemics. The unity of the bloc needed sincere consultations. The article criticized the Chinese for the violence with which they expressed their views and adopted without any hesitation the main Soviet line of peaceful coexistence and nuclear disarmament; but on the other hand it reiterated more emphatically than ever before the by then already well-known Rumanian theme of the 'abolition of the capitalist division of labour between advanced industrial countries and backward agricultural ones'; and it repeated again that full and unfettered sovereignty of the member countries was the only basis for the progress and work of COMECON.

The next step was the visit of a Rumanian delegation to Pekin in March 1964, headed by Maurer, for 'ideological discussions' with a delegation headed by Liu Chao-shi. The visit seems to have been fruitless; but on his way back Maurer went to the Crimea to see Khrushchev, thus asserting his position as an 'honest broker'. Later the Rumanian intervention was acknowledged by the CPSU as having formed a distinct stage in the quarrel – and having been the cause of a temporary but useless truce in the polemics.

On 26 April 1964 the Rumanian Workers' Party published a long and painstaking 'declaration' on all important ideological matters – the first complete Rumanian doctrinal text of this calibre. The declaration's general pronouncements were once again ambivalent. It recognized that the general international line of peaceful coexistence and disarmament, taken by the Soviet Union, was the best for the Communist camp. Moreover, for the first time, the Rumanian Workers' Party recanted its previous approval of the exclusion from the Cominform and the family of Communist Parties of the Yugoslav League of Communists. But long parts of the declaration, dealing with relations between socialist countries within COMECON and with relations between parties, were unprecedentedly outspoken and couched in a new style of doctrinal authority previously unknown in the Rumanian Workers' Party. The rejection of the 'unique planning body', which had been personally put forward by Khrushchev in the autumn of 1962, was this time explicit and uncompromising. The sovereignty of the socialist State requires that it should hold in its own hands all the levers and controls of the national economic life, said the declaration. 'To transfer any such commands to some supra-national or extra-national organs would be to empty the notion of sovereignty of all its contents.'

Two further objections were forcefully made against the integrationist tendencies of the other countries of COMECON. The principle of total sovereignty was extended to the 'inter-states unions or branches of technical production as well as to the mixed companies which could be the common property of two or more States . . .' 'The State plan is unique and indivisible, and parts or sections of it cannot be taken out of the control of the State.' And a strong reminder was included that as long as COMECON itself only comprised eight of the fourteen Communist-governed countries in the world it could only be described as a 'partial organization'. In order to give real validity to its decisions and plans it should comprise all socialist countries and even countries which showed a marked tendency to adopt socialist institutions and patterns. This of course would have amounted to the dissolution of COMECON as a regional economic unit.

Regarding relations between parties, the declaration took a characteristically 'polycentric' stand. 'All parties', it said, 'enjoy equal rights on the principle of non-interference in other parties' domestic affairs, on each party's exclusive rights to solve its own political and organizational problem of appointing leadership and of giving its members the proper guidance in problems of cultural and international politics.' (This paragraph produced an immediate Russian reaction. Radio Moscow announced soon after that it had reduced some of its foreign broadcasts, but broadcasts to China, Cuba and Rumania were in fact increased.)

Once Rumania's pragmatist position was established (and it is clear that the 'declaration' will serve as an ideological basis for the duration of the present leadership of the Rumanian Workers' Party) it became easier for the Rumanian Workers' Party to go ahead with their own pragmatic political approaches.

The first step, taken before, during and after the crisis with COMECON, was to reopen many of the links between Rumania and the West. These links had been the bloodstream of Rumanian history. Here again therefore the Rumanian Workers' Party achieved a double object. Such a move was not only the most natural way to circumvent a possible COMECON blockade of Rumania, which could paralyse her ambitious plans for industrialization, but it was also very popular with the Rumanian people. Moreover, the Rumanians in this respect aroused the envy of all the other Eastern Europeans. The Western countries responded promptly and intelligently. Rumanian trade delegations were received with sympathy. Contracts were signed without difficulty. At the beginning they were limited to secondary and minor industrial plants. But soon they were extended to cover the requirements of some of the main sections of the plans for industrialization for which the 'Communist family' either could not deliver the goods, or even if it could, refused to do so in order to curb Rumanian ambitions. In some cases, long-term credits were granted, although Rumania, because of her natural resources, was not so insistent as other Communist countries on this point. In May 1964 during high-level economic negotiations with the US in Washington the Rumanian delegation asked that Rumania should be granted the status of the 'most favoured nation'. In many cases technical help was provided. The new Rumanian industries were able to use the services of British, French, Italian, West German and American engineers and technicians, who replaced the perennial Russians. Besides, the Governments of these countries insisted on broadening more than just their trade relations with Rumania. Cultural exchanges were fostered with less enthusiasm by the Rumanian Government than by the old and new intellectuals and *élites*, who implemented and enlarged them with obvious impatience. Tourists were encouraged to visit the country, and Rumanians to travel abroad. Visas and passports were more freely granted. Bucharest and the Rumanian holiday resorts assumed again some of the cosmopolitan glamour for which they were famous before the war.

But pragmatism is contagious and it spreads quickly from one sector to another. The Rumanians had been unflinching partisans of Khrushchev's policy of peaceful coexistence with the capitalist West since its inception. But they now made it clear that this policy too could be 'polycentric' – in the sense that each Communist country could have its own direct relations with Western countries and sometimes even its own point of view in international deliberations. In many instances, the delegation of the Rumanian People's Republic at the United Nations European Economic Commission or in some other committees and councils took a stand and expressed opinions differing from those of the Soviet bloc, and was eager to propose more flexibility in all international exchanges. In September 1963 the Rumanians voted at the UN with the West and against the Soviet bloc on the issue of the denuclearized zone in Latin America.

The State visit of the Prime Minister, Maurer, to Paris in October 1964 was another and spectacular demonstration of the new Rumanian prestige and nonconformism. In his statements after his talks with General de Gaulle and the French Prime Minister and Minister of External Affairs, Maurer stressed the need for closer cooperation between countries with independent outlooks which put above all other considerations the mutual respect for sovereignty and international equality. The frequent complimentary allusions made by each side to the independent attitude shown by the other were not made only for the sake of emphasizing the point. The Rumanian Communists may have admired de Gaulle's show of independence within the Western alliance; and de Gaulle may have thought that the effort of the 'little Latin sister' from the East to assert some independence with the Communist bloc deserved encouragement and sympathy. Flexibility in international affairs, with a view to attaining newer and more up-to-date points of view and policies than those so deeply shaped in the shadow of the conflict of the two blocs led by the two Super-Powers, is the avowed quest of statesmen of such diverse aims and methods as de Gaulle, Tito, Harold Wilson, Castro or Willi Brandt and of the Scandinavian, Austrian and Swiss leading political parties. The Rumanian Workers' Party was adding for the first time to this concert the voice of a country from within the Soviet bloc and the Warsaw Treaty organization.

The *rapprochement* between the dogmatist Rumanians and the revisionist Yugoslavs which took place at remarkable speed was not only one more substantial proof of their pragmatic approach. It was also very probably one of the deepest and most influential developments in that area. From an ideological point of view the Yugoslav League and the Polish party (both having practically dropped collectivization), or the Yugoslav League and the Hungarian party (which both deliberately underplay their part in the life of the State so as to make themselves more acceptable to the intelligentsia and the workers), have more in common than the Yugoslav League and the Rumanian Workers' Party. The latter hurried to achieve full collectivization in April 1962 – three years ahead of the plan. It is an ardent believer in 'speedy' heavy industrialization, reminiscent from many points of view of the Stalinist industrialization undertaken by sacrificing the consumer goods industry and by setting high productivity and investment targets; and it excludes any foreseeable withering away of and change in the structure of the dictatorship of the proletariat.

On all these three main points, on which the Rumanians are most backward, the Yugoslavs are most advanced. Yet it is with Yugoslavia that Rumania has, since her emancipation from the very close embrace of the Soviet Union and of the Soviet bloc, achieved the deepest and most fertile collaboration. This is, of course, partly explained by the unclouded friendship between the two countries, both having attained full territorial integrity after the First World War; both having been partners in the Little Entente; neither having ever fought a war against the other (Rumania, unlike Hungary and Bulgaria, refused Hitler's injunction to follow his punitive expedition against Yugoslavia on 27 March 1941).

But above all the explanation of this friendship can be found in the geo-political importance of the closeness of the two countries. Rumania forms the greatest part of the territory between Yugoslavia and Soviet Russia; while Yugoslavia is for Rumania the only neighbouring country which is not a member of either the Warsaw Treaty military organization or of COMECON – and it forms a bridge with the Mediterranean and the West.

Another factor which draws the two countries together is that the Yugoslav and Rumanian Communists have now in common a firm determination to prevent Soviet Russia from bringing them to heel again. The opening-up of relations with the West is one of the practical corollaries of this political concern in both countries. Another is the quest for closer collaboration between the two, and any other East European Communist country, with a view to the creation of some regional political or diplomatic grouping of their own. The vast common economic projects launched in May 1963; the exceptionally friendly and in many respects unique reception given by the Yugoslavs to Gheorghiu-Dej in October 1963; and the frequent consultations between the two leaders during 1964, the year of Khrushchev's final attempt to break the deadlock created in the world Communist movement by the Sino–Soviet conflict – all these and many other manifestations were the signs of the constant deepening and broadening of the relations between the two Governments.

By the summer of 1964 the rhythm of events in the Communist world was gathering momentum as the Communist parties were asked to take their stand on the Soviet invitation to the preparatory conference in which the controversy with the Chinese would be brought to an end, one way or the other. Yet when on 15 June 1964 the CPSU took the decision to risk the final meeting as a means of stopping the rot of 'schismatism' by a showdown, it was not because the CPSU's position in the struggle had improved. On the contrary, the situation from the CPSU's point of view had deteriorated further and the decision was, as it were, the admission of the need for surgery before the damage was beyond repair. Once, a year before, in October 1963, the CPSU had obviously come to the same conclusion – and seemed to be on the point of launching an appeal for the calling of the conference. But ominous responses, some public, like that of the Norwegian Communist Party in October 1963 declaring that it 'would not participate in the discussion in a manner which might result in the further sharpening and deterioration of the situation', and some more confidential replies, like the Polish and Italian calls for caution, had caused the CPSU in 1963 to postpone the move and to wait for a better opportunity. But in the light of the increased aggressiveness of the Chinese and Albanian parties, Khrushchev, who during 1964 had been personally attacked with greater virulence than ever before and who was faced with the rapid progress of Chinese factionalism in the movement at large, evidently decided to risk a showdown. He must have known that he would face perhaps greater difficulties than the previous year; but obviously he thought that with some manoeuvring and pressure the CPSU would once more carry the day:

The time is ripe for representatives of the Marxist–Leninist parties to meet. A majority of fraternal parties regard the calling of such a conference as necessary. But some leaders in the fraternal parties express doubts as to whether such a meeting would do any good in the present conditions. . . . We call upon all communist and workers' parties to pool their efforts in the struggle for the common cause. In order to consolidate our unity, it will be useful to call a conference to discuss all issues confronting the world communist movement. We believe that all truly Marxist–Leninist parties and all revolutionary parties will overcome the difficulties created by the action of the splitters.

This was one of his last statements on this matter during his visit to Czechoslovakia in September 1964.

On 10 August *Pravda* published the news that an invitation

had been issued by the CPSU to the twenty-six parties which
had taken part in the preparatory conference of 1960 to meet
again in Moscow on 15 December 1964. The parties were the
Albanian, American, Argentinian, Australian, Brazilian,
British, Bulgarian, Chinese, Cuban, Czechoslovak, East
German, West German, Finnish, French, Hungarian, Indian,
Indonesian, Italian, Japanese, Mongolian, North Korean,
Polish, Rumanian, Syrian, Soviet Russian and North Vietnamese. All the Communist parties and particularly the twenty-
six invited to the conference were now faced with the moment
of truth. The Russians were asking them to attend and the
Chinese were refusing with more violence than ever even to
consider the idea of a conference, which for them was only a
manoeuvre to split the movement right open. The other parties
were now being forced to show openly with whom they sided
and whose wrath they were going to arouse. Moreover, both
Super-Parties started at once to canvass their supporters. The
Chinese immediately gained an advantage among the Asian
parties, which, with the Albanians in Europe, announced early
in the day their refusal to attend. The CPSU and Khrushchev
personally hoped to persuade the European parties, and above
all the East European ones, to come to the fateful rendezvous.

East and West reacted differently. The Chinese were soon
firmly in control of the greater number of the parties 'friendly'
to them. But the parties which the Soviet Union might have
hoped to count on for support showed conflicting attitudes. It
was the Italian party which took upon itself the task of dis-
agreeing publicly with the CPSU and of convincing the other
parties of the dangers implicit in the Russian move. By means of
the Press and the publications of this most exuberant of the
European parties and by means of a round of visits made by
Togliatti, Longo, Pajetta and other leaders to the fraternal
parties, the Italians publicly denounced the danger of taking
decisions affecting the unity of the world Communist movement
at a hurried and uncompromising meeting. But without insisting too much in public they also hinted at the danger of allowing a new 'single centre' controlled by the CPSU to be re-
constituted. The European, and generally speaking all the other

Communist parties which had, since Stalin's death, freed themselves as much as possible from the control of a centralized leadership, might, they implied, be brought back under it for the sake of the 'united fight against the dogmatists', as they had been brought in 1948 under the control of Cominform under the pretext of the 'united fight against the Titoists'. As Togliatti put it in the memorandum which became after his death on 23 August his 'testament':

> We are opposed to any kind of suggestion that a new central international organization should be created. We reaffirm the unity of our movement and of the international workers' movement but this unity must be achieved within the difference of the concrete political positions corresponding to the situation and to the degree of evolution of each country.

Togliatti and the Italians were talking for many other European parties (some of which, like the Norwegian, did not mince their words either) and for the East European parties which feared that the Russians might reconstitute an international centre. The point was lucidly put in an Albanian article of 13 November 1964:

> The testament of Togliatti points out that now at least two different lines of tactics in the struggle against Marxism–Leninism are taking shape: the 'monocentrist' line of the Khrushchev group and the 'polycentrist' line of Togliatti. . . . The contradictions between the Khrushchevites and the Italian polycentrist revisionists are the most pronounced. These two tendencies are opposed on the subject of the Khrushchevite plan to convene an international meeting of communist and workers' parties.

And the Albanian article was not slow to point to the third player in the game, the usual *bête noire* of Tirana: the Yugoslavs.

> The Tito element is trying to encourage and deepen the differences which were born within revisionism and to weaken the domination of the Khrushchev group over its partners.

In spite of their obsessive concern with Yugoslavia the

Albanians were this time not far from the truth. Since the announcement in June that the conference at which the issue was to be decided was to be held in the near future, the parties of the Soviet bloc, subjected to the contradictory persuasions of the Russians and the Italians, had shown a tendency to consult with Tito. On 24 June Tito had talks with Dej; on 26 June with Gomulka; on 15 September with Kádár; on 21 September with Novotny; on 25 September with Ulbricht.

Never before, not even after the Canossa of 1955, did Tito receive such an open confirmation of the instinctive hope of the other East European parties that they could find through the more far-sighted Yugoslavs some way of holding together without being propped up by the Russians and thus achieve a new and different unity. This was not merely due to the storm descending over the world Communist movement because of Khrushchev's untimely call for a showdown with China. It was a sign of the long-repressed and yet always resurgent tendency towards an Eastern European Communist regrouping of some kind which would differentiate the parties and countries of Eastern Europe from and protect them against the Great Power, Soviet Russia. Tito's journey through Eastern Europe during June had followed an itinerary which had at least a symbolic meaning since it extended from Finland in the north down to Poland and Rumania; and in September he consulted with the leaders of Hungary, Czechoslovakia and East Germany. The 'tier of middle States' recurred again in this itinerary and the visits and counter-visits were reminiscent of those undertaken by him in 1946–7 when the idea of some East European federation was so much in the air that it provoked an immediate and brutal Russian reaction. Since then, though, Tito had openly proclaimed, through his intensive collaboration with the neutralist non-European States and especially with India and the United Arab Republic, his doctrine of the common interest of the 'non-aligned' and the 'anti-bloc' countries – and in 1956 it was this doctrine which guided the Hungarian Communist Party under Nagy's leadership and reintroduced the idea of neutrality with such an explosive force in the political arsenal of Communist Eastern Europe.

G

In the Soviet bloc the Rumanian Workers' Party took the most open stand against Khrushchev's plan to hold a conference. Through various 'leakages' and 'official sources' (as for instance some replies made by the Rumanian ambassadors in Paris, Vienna and Budapest) it announced that it would refuse to attend the meeting, if indeed the meeting was ever going to be held. While the other parties, and especially the Hungarian, Bulgarian and Czechoslovak, issued frequent statements in favour of the holding of the conference, the Rumanian Workers' Party media of communication referred constantly to its earlier statements asking for caution, bilateral exchanges between the CCP and the CPSU, and above all for the non-interference under any guise of a party in the right of decision of other parties. Later it was confirmed that, when the meeting was held, the Rumanian Workers' Party did not go, and was the only bloc party which refused to attend the meeting. Less than a month later Gheorghiv-Dej died, and it is more than probable that his successor will continue the same line of resolute independence in these matters.

But the other Eastern European parties also, in spite of the more or less vociferous backing they were giving, under pressure, to Khrushchev, shared many of the Rumanians' apprehensions. The Polish party, for one, although on paper it took a line of solidarity with the CPSU, was pleading in more secret correspondence for the postponement of the meeting and for the settling of the dispute on the lines indicated by the Italians. The same views were shared by the other parties, although in public statements they chose to keep as near to Khrushchev as possible. Thus the CPSU was faced with the daunting fact that if it forced the issue it might have some expected and some unexpected defections even in the very heart of the Soviet bloc parties; and that, partly because of the Sino–Soviet conflict, the new 'Communist neutralism' was making new progress in Eastern Europe.

As 15 December drew nearer, and the Communist parties were plumbing the bitter depths of their 'agonizing reappraisals', it was announced from Moscow on 15 October 1964 that Khrushchev had been dismissed. It is beyond the province of this work, and in any case too early in the day, to assess fully the significance of this event. It came as a surprise to world public opinion, for Khrushchev in the last decade had been the intriguing protagonist of a Soviet policy in which, for once, it was difficult to distinguish between the old ruses of Soviet revolutionary hypocrisy and the new humanistic accents of a mellowed Soviet society. It came as a greater surprise still to those sovietologists of the free world who had never believed that the Soviet establishment could generate an opposition powerful enough to dethrone whoever had installed himself in the seat of power; and who now, like so many other people, could not believe that this was precisely what had happened. Besides, there were so many trends converging in this one single political event, from the internal economic to the external ideological and diplomatic ones, that time was needed to collect the evidence on which to base a post-mortem.

But by intuition as well as by logic, it was generally assumed that Khrushchev had been sacrificed for the series of failures suffered by Soviet Russia during his tenure of power. The Soviet establishment reacted, like all elemental political groups, in the classical way described by Sir James Frazer, the anthropologist, under the title of 'how kings are killed when strength fails', and by Machiavelli, the political philosopher, in the famous maxim that 'conspirators always believe that the death of a prince will be to the benefit of the people'. Sometimes such healthy superstitions stop progressive decay; sometimes they only spark off the internal convulsions of a ruling group haunted by its own ill-luck and lead to further disintegration.

In the conclusions of this survey of the relations between Soviet Russia and the East European people's democracies an attempt will be made to describe in broad terms the perspective which might open up after Khrushchev's fall, but two more facts must be recorded first. One is that the Eastern European parties which had played an outstanding part in the three successive defeats inflicted on the prestige and authority of the CPSU in the last fifteen years or so played also an undeniable part in the last crisis. The CPSU discovered that once again it must fight on two fronts in the ideological battle, on its Eastern as well as on its Western one, and that whatever the basic differences between the dogmatists and the revisionists, polycentrists and monocentrists, all parties were united in their determination not to allow the CPSU to bring them back under the control from which all had suffered for more than forty years. This influenced its decision to postpone and possibly avoid the engagement; and to dismiss the man who had been most associated with it. The authority of the CPSU was for the first time challenged and denied in Eastern Europe with the rebellion of the Yugoslav 'revisionists'. And it was Eastern Europe again which refused to help the CPSU in its effort to reassert its authority, whatever the reasons or pretexts. The CPSU had taken the decision to engage the final battle with the Chinese, when Khrushchev was convinced that it would be backed by the European and especially by the Eastern European parties. The CPSU dismissed Khrushchev for, among other reasons, having been proved wrong in this respect.

The second fact is that the manner of Khrushchev's fall shocked the European and Eastern European peoples. It was in their eyes a further proof of the arbitrariness and unreliability of political conditions in the Soviet Union. While the East European 'ruling parties' conducted their inquiries more silently, the West European parties, led again by the Italians, but this time followed by the British, French, Norwegian, Austrian and practically all the other parties, expressed their dismay at the way in which political problems of this magnitude were still solved in the Soviet Union. An unprecedented and indeed inconceivable procession of party delegations went to Moscow to ask for explanations – and came back barely satisfied with the embarrassed accounts given by the 'new leadership'.

In the Eastern European camp the Hungarian, Czechoslovak and Polish parties, which had questioned the procedure openly, afterwards accepted unenthusiastically the reasons given in Moscow. But neither Tito, nor Gheorghiu-Dej, of whom it had always been said that he was not going to Moscow because of his personal dislike of Khrushchev, attended the celebrations of the November revolution – nor did they attend the subsequent ideological gathering which was held in Moscow on the occasion of the first official visit of the Chinese party since the split occurred. There were no signs of whole-hearted approval or of a change in the attitude of aloofness lately shown by the Eastern European parties. It remains to be seen whether the 'new leadership' will continue to show to the Yugoslavs the same friendship which Khrushchev showed to them since 1959 and whether, in order to placate the Chinese and also to stop the revisionist rot from spreading still farther, the CPSU will not try to propose new 'platforms' in which once more dogmatism and revisionism will both be criticized. This secondary trend will be worth watching, especially because of the reactions it may cause in the leadership of the other East European Communist parties. But there is no doubt that the primary effect of Khrushchev's dismissal and of the uncertainties to which it gave birth had been to aggravate the East European Communist parties' distrust of the CPSU and confirmed them in their strong new orientation towards further 'disengagement' from their old links with the CPSU and towards new, and from all points of view more neutral, positions.

Conclusions

In the introduction we justified the expression 'Soviet Empire'. Now that the history of this empire has been retraced it only remains to see how far it is fair to speak of a 'break-up'. Does what has happened to the zone of Soviet military, economic and ideological domination in Eastern Europe amount to a 'disintegration, decay, collapse, dispersal'?*

From an ideological point of view, the most recent events, as described and interpreted by the communist media themselves, provide the most conclusive proof. The 'disintegration' or 'dispersal' of the CPSU's authority as set up by Lenin and consolidated by Stalin over the entire communist movement, including the Soviet bloc in Eastern Europe, is now a fact. The communiqué issued at the end of the abortive conference of the nineteen communist parties on 1–5 March 1965 was a most humiliating occasion for the Soviet Union and a veritable funeral oration for communist authority.

The introductory paragraph, listing the parties which attended the meeting, already showed how the authority of Lenin and Stalin, and even of Khrushchev, had diminished under Brezhnev and Kosygin. The two new leaders had of course done their utmost to persuade all the twenty-six parties, if not to adopt the Soviet point of view, at least to attend the meeting. Humiliating visits were paid to the Chinese, North Vietnamese and North Korean parties; special inducements were held out to them, including a promise given and kept by the CPSU that the meeting would be of an entirely different nature from that contemplated by Khrushchev when he first called it in August 1964. Khrushchev had probably intended to face the parties thus assembled with definite alternatives, culminating in the excommunication of the Chinese. Brezhnev and Kosygin wanted merely to re-unite

*Oxford English Dictionary.

the parties around pious formulas of solidarity acceptable to all. From Asia they received a dusty answer. Not only did the parties ignore the invitation to attend the conference, but on the very eve of the meeting the Chinese press launched a broadside against the CPSU. 'Khrushchevism without Khrushchev' was the verdict of Peking and Tirana on the pólicy of the new Russian leaders. Moreover the Chinese, adding insult to injury, republished in full Khrushchev's principal speeches, now banned by his successors in Soviet Russia.

In the Eastern European family, the Rumanian party stuck adamantly to its initial (April 1964) threat. If the two belligerent parties could not solve their differences beforehand, the RWP would not side with either. This stand showed more than anything else how widespread was the 'disintegration, decay, collapse and dispersal' of the Soviet party's former authority in ideological questions, even among the parties nearest to them. The Rumanian Workers' Party refused to send a delegation. It refused to send observers, as the American party did, or even to go at the last moment, under obviously strong emotional strain, as the British Communist Party did.

But in one sense, those parties which did attend the conference did the CPSU an even greater disservice. For their participation (and probably the Italian and Polish parties played the leading part here) caused the mighty CPSU itself to sign the death warrant of its own former ideological hegemony and leadership. The communiqué started with the open confession that between the communist parties of the world 'there are differences over the political line and over many important problems of *theory and tactics*' (our italics). It had no remedies to offer for this depressing situation other than two poor panaceas. One was a recommendation that open polemics should be discontinued and replaced by fraternal exchanges of opinion on the various problems of 'theory and tactics' at stake. The other was the intimation that the task lying ahead for the revolutionary parties of the world was 'to consolidate' the positions of socialism.

Nothing could reveal more clearly how low were the new targets of the former leading party, or the risk it ran of presenting an old and dispirited image to the new African and Asian parties in contrast with the 'fervent' Chinese. But the main reason for this abdication can be found in another sentence of the communiqué – a sentence which cannot possibly have been inspired by the CPSU, for whom it is indeed the death knell. 'The participants at the meeting', it ran 'favour a strict observance of the rules for relations between parties which were laid down by the Conferences of 1957 and 1960, and are against the interference by any party in the internal affairs of other parties.' In the light of this, the entire text becomes an outstanding admission by the world communist movement, not only that it has put an end to the CPSU's leadership, but also that this leadership has not been replaced by any other. The plain truth is that henceforth there will be no ideological centre or line binding for any party, even for those of the Soviet bloc in eastern Europe. In its flat declaration of dissolution the communiqué resembled if anything Togliatti's posthumous message of August 1964. It, too, is a 'testament'. But while Togliatti spoke of 'polycentrism', what emerged now is a-centrism. There is no centre.

From an economic point of view, the dissolution of the bloc is progressing rapidly, both in the internal, doctrinal plane and in the external plane of foreign trade. The most remarkable event was the somersault of the Czechoslovak party and government. Formerly the most dogmatic and pedantic imitators of the CPSU and of its economic doctrine, the Czechs in the last half of 1964 made a complete *volte face*. The party first confessed publicly that for fifteen years it had committed the grave mistake of copying the Soviet model and imposing it on the different realities of Czechoslovakia. It then admitted that the Yugoslav example was in fact the most relevant and suitable, and declared that from these premisses of flexibility and spontaneity in domestic economy and in trade, Communist Czechoslovakia could build up its own new and more appropriate set of economic rules.

As a result Czechoslovak planning is by now the freest and most dynamic in the entire bloc. It insists on the virtue of private initiative in enterprises, on continuous de-centralization from the control of the ministries in Prague, on non-interference of party and state in the management of factories and businesses, and on incentives to producers, both in industry and agriculture. In consequence the Czechoslovak administration is in *practice* more advanced than the Soviet Professor Liberman, still a lonely voice in Russia, is in *theory*.

It remains to be seen, of course, how far this process of loosening the economic strings can go in a régime which is politically still very rigid. This is precisely the 'fundamental dilemma'* which faces the revisionist communist governments. But the fact is that now even Czechoslovakia, a last bastion of Marxist–Leninist economic orthodoxy, has yielded to the pressure for liberal and national improvisations, a pressure long since accepted in Yugoslavia, Poland, Hungary and lately in Rumania and even Bulgaria.

As far as regional discipline under the aegis of the CPSU is concerned, it has become more and more evident that COMECON will remain a dead duck. Moves were made, especially on Polish and Hungarian initiative, to continue further integration of the economies, without – or even perhaps to spite – the Rumanian Workers' Party. (For instance the creation of INTERMETAL, an organization linking the steel industries of Poland, Hungary and East Germany.) But the tendency among members of COMECON to increase their trade with the non-communist markets is constantly growing. The most amazing instance of this remains the promise of future collaboration between Gomulka's Poland and the big West German concern, Krupp, of Essen. This entails the setting up by Krupp on Polish territory of industrial plants and factories in which imported raw materials will be manufactured by Polish workers and the goods re-exported to West Germany and to other non-communist markets. In any circumstances the formation by communist states and capitalist firms of such mixed companies would seem odd. (It was known that during the economic negotiations between communist Rumania and the United States in 1964, the Rumanian delegation had offered to set up with American firms such mixed companies.) Even more surprising is that this time

* The expression used by Professor Mihal Markovic of Belgrade University.

the capitalist concern involved is Krupp, a name which in the world at large and in Eastern Europe in particular still bears the fearful reputation of having been the main armament factory for the Kaiser's and Hitler's wars of aggression. The fact that the communist country which is now prepared to consider such a collaboration is Poland, which suffered most from German aggression, and where communist propaganda's most effective weapon is still fear of Germany, makes the proposed deal even more significant.

It vividly demonstrates two things. On the one hand it shows how non-conformist and pragmatic the Soviet bloc countries can now be in the field of foreign trade. On the other it shows how acutely they must need to tap the financial and industrial resources of the West, whence alone they can hope to acquire what is unavailable in the pool of COMECON but is needed to develop the overall economic resources of the bloc as a whole. While criticizing the Rumanian Party and Government for the unorthodox trade policies they have adopted since 1960, the Poles, Czechoslovaks, Hungarians and indeed the East Germans have tried hard in the last five years to emulate and, if possible, to outdo them in their successful overtures to the West. In the economic sector, too, centrifugalism has come to stay.

There remains the military sphere. Here collaboration between the Peoples' Democracies and Soviet Russia is more stable (though other spheres are bound to influence trends to some extent) for two reasons. First, the communist parties in power in all these countries are anxious to preserve the myth that the entire region is united under the friendly wing of the first communist state in world history – Soviet Russia. It is clear that all the adaptations, reforms and national variations introduced by the communist governments of Eastern Europe have been in response to popular pressure; and the greater a government's sensitivity to this native pressure, the prompter its effort to find some compromise between the Russian Leninist–Stalinist models and the national reality. Sooner or later, though, all the communist parties of Eastern Europe had buttressed popular support for themselves by stressing their particular value as intermediants between Russia and their own peoples. Yet the governments remain aware that Russia's influence over the whole region is indispensable for them if they are to maintain power; and therefore they believe that while they should acquire for themselves as much freedom as possible in order to make their administrations smoother, more efficient and more palatable, they are nevertheless ultimately linked with the Soviet Union, her fate and her evolution by a basic common problem.

This problem is the 'fundamental dilemma' of any communist state: how to enable the people to participate in the decision-making process in the life of the state, without once more being drawn irresistibly into the obvious institutions of free elections and multi-party systems which could lead to the loss of power of the 'monolithic' party. In developed industrial or semi-industrial societies, the multiple influences of the component groups in society are bound to conflict with the monolithic party and its rule. The problem of representation and of participation in the debate on the nation's economic life without a corresponding participation in the debate on political life creates the 'dilemma' common to all these states. From the Soviet Union as the conservative archetype to Yugoslavia as the most advanced and boldest innovator in various experiments and compromises, the communist governments in Europe must all walk the same tightrope. This is perhaps what unites the communist governments most closely with that of the Soviet Union. Each of them is trying separately and will continue to try to work out some device by which the dictatorship of the monolithic party can 'wither away' and transmute itself into 'the state of the whole people', which has already been proclaimed to be in existence since the 22nd Congress and yet is still indistinguishable from the mixture as before.

The second reason for the stability of the military collaboration between the eastern European countries and the Soviet Union is that the Soviet Union still carefully maintains the overall military control of the area which it established by the Warsaw Treaty. As has been shown earlier, at the height of the trend to de-Stalinize and bring new flexibility into the relations between the USSR and the former Stalinist satellites, the leaders of the USSR always clung to the Warsaw Treaty Organization as the main instrument of their political, diplomatic and strategic influence in Europe. To the USSR the issue is a simple strategic one. It has to maintain its communications with its military base in Europe, East Germany, as free and elastic as possible. The *de facto* military control of the area by the Soviet Union and her firmness in maintaining it have ensured a stable situation hitherto, regardless of East European views. On the other hand, the natural instinct of the East European nations is to try to attain a status of neutrality comparable in some respects to that of Austria or Finland, or to Yugoslavia's neutralism. (A distinction must however be drawn here. Though it may be true to say that all the peoples of Eastern Europe regard the possibility of achieving neutral status as one of their principal political aspirations, the same is not true of all the communist governments.)

The past history of their relations with Germany enables the Polish and Czech governments to keep alive in their peoples an awareness that the alliance with the Soviet Union and the other countries of the Soviet bloc is a welcome safeguard against the dangers of their vicinity with *any* kind of Germany. But the Hungarian or Bulgarian or even Rumanian communist governments have less reason to 'fear' the West. Recent developments have shown Kadar conjuring up the possibility under some conditions of the withdrawal of Soviet troops from Hungary. And Rumania, on her own, has taken the unprecedented step of reducing the duration of military service, which in all the Warsaw treaty countries lasts for two years, to sixteen months. By this solitary move the Rumanian communist government has shown that fear of military aggression from the West will not inspire it to increase its military expenditure and deprive its industrial development of the massive contingents of manpower kept in the forces. It is here, in the obscure realm of their relations with the Warsaw treaty organization, that the next round between the more centrifugal communist governments and the Soviet government will be played out. It is here that the new definitions of 'national sovereignty' and of 'the communist commonwealth' will probably be tested.

The Warsaw treaty organization is the last survivor of Stalin's attempt to build up a Soviet Empire in Eastern Europe. The communist governments, in their quest for fuller sovereignty, realize that this is now the main obstacle in their path, for the issue of war and peace is not under their ultimate control, and the representative of the Soviet Union is the ultimate commander of their military forces. It is also here that the Soviet Union shows the greatest obduracy; and the fact that Imre Nagy fell between the clamour of the people for neutrality and the adamant refusal of the Soviet Union to consider allowing Hungary to leave the Warsaw treaty organization provides a measure of the extent of the conflict.

Can the Soviet Union accept that it is possible for a communist commonwealth to survive in Europe, without its members being subordinate, even in military matters, to the dominating power? And will other members of the commonwealth join Yugoslavia, non-aligned between the military blocs of the world, even if this further undermines the USSR's old Stalinist precepts: Soviet military security based on the creation of this pivotal buffer zone and jumping-off board? Finally, bearing in mind that except in East Germany – the last, and perhaps by now crumbling, bastion of Stalin's empire – all the other zones of Russian influence have undergone profound changes, can we now say that Stalin's empire has indeed broken up?

The answers must be yes. Indeed, it is inconceivable that, in any circumstances, Soviet Russia could have built a lasting empire in a part of Europe which by its very nature is a cradle of nationalism and a permanent cause of conflict of interests between the powers of the world. The years of Stalin's truly imperial rule over these peoples were short, violent and precarious; the failure was implicit in the attempt.

Appendix

A Note On The Historical Importance Of Eastern Europe

As a whole Eastern Europe is that part of the continent which stretches between the four seas: the Adriatic to the south-west; the Aegean and the Black Sea to the south-east; the Mediterranean to the south and the Baltic to the north. For the purpose of this book this definition comprehends the present Communist Eastern Europe, omitting only Greece.

The Eastern Europe which is projected here from a historical point of view is that which was created in 1878, by the Congress of Berlin. It is true that many things have changed. The greatest political forces in the world are now extra-European, the United States and Soviet Russia. The old local pattern of interests, those of Austria–Hungary, the Ottoman Empire and Tsarist Russia,* has disappeared for good. The Versailles settlement of 1919 filled the vacuum with small national or even ethnic States, some of which have survived. The Germany of Bismarck is now divided and the Western part comes into the picture only as an important member of what is now called the West or NATO. But all this being said, there are still two crucial planes on which the basic Eastern European political parallelogram of forces, as drawn in the Congress of Berlin in 1878, remains unchanged.

The first plane is formed by the conflicting aims of East and West. The Western Powers, were – and still are – interested in uniting the whole continent homogeneously and in keeping Eastern Europe open as a route to the Middle East and Asia; Russia, as an Eastern Power, was – and still is – interested in enlarging her territorial advance to the west and south as far as possible. The main Russian–German line of cleavage, still today Europe's most dangerous cleft, was first drawn in 1878,

* It must be remembered here that at that time Poland, which had been a power in north-eastern Europe, had been partitioned and mostly absorbed by Russia.

when Bismarck strengthened the German–Austrian alliance. At the same time, the Berlin settlement crystallized further the positions of the Powers in the 'Eastern question', a triangular conflict of interests in south-east Europe between the decaying Ottoman Empire, the messianic Tsarist Empire, and the Western Powers eager to penetrate into the hitherto hermetically sealed region. So, roughly speaking, the Western Powers and Russia were facing each other, then as now, suspicious and hostile across two disputed zones: one of these created in the north by divided Poland and the other created in the south by the imminent collapse of the Turkish empire in Europe.

The second crucial factor surviving from 1878 is a result of the struggle between the Eastern Powers and the rising peoples of the region, who were legitimately the heirs of the oppressor empires. Poles in Poland, Czechoslovaks in Bohemia and Slovakia, Hungarians in Austro-Hungary, Rumanians in Wallachia, Moldavia, Transylvania, Bessarabia and Bukovina, Bulgarians in Bulgaria and Rumelia, Yugoslavs in Serbia, Croatia and Slovenia – all those were fighting a blind but unrelenting fight against one of the three empires or sometimes two or even three together.

In this fight they were encouraged for moral and political reasons by the Western Powers: Gladstone, Napoleon III, Bismarck himself set the high moral tone of the West's attitude towards the 'fight for national freedom of the young European (or even Christian) peoples' of Eastern Europe. The gradual, if patchy, emancipation of larger and larger parts of the region was brought about by one European conference or congress after another – with the constant help of the Western chancelleries, in their turn urged on by public opinion in their countries. Western historians strengthened the nationalist theories of the rising peoples by their writing, confirming their presence in the respective territories even before the Asiatic migrations; as well as their tortured existence as European marches and battlefields against Asia. The leaders of the national movements in each of these countries drew their inspiration and help from France, Britain and even Germany. At the same time, the Western Powers competed between themselves in the new embryo States

for markets and raw materials, capital investments and concessions. From this more or less triangular entanglement in
Eastern Europe sprang two world wars: that of 1914–18
in south-east Europe over Serbia, and that of 1939–45 in
north-east Europe over Poland. The Nazi–Soviet war of 1941
also sprang from Eastern Europe when the two accomplices
found it impossible to trust each other's intentions in that
region.

There can be no doubt that Eastern Europe has played an
important part in the political development of the world in the
nineteenth and twentieth centuries. The twentieth-century geo-
politician H. J. Mackinder, who was also a Member of Parliament and an expert in the British delegation to the Peace
Conference of 1919–21, was, even more strongly than his
German colleagues, convinced that the peace of Europe and of
the world was dependent on finding a long-lasting if not permanent settlement of the Eastern European problem. (The German
and the British geo-politicians of course proposed diametrically
opposite solutions.) Mackinder's main theory can be found in
the following passage which, written at the end of the First
World War, has an ominously prophetic ring when read after
the Second:

It is essential that we should focus our thoughts on the stable
resettlement of the affairs of East Europe and the Heartland. If we
accept anything less than a complete solution of the Eastern question
in its largest sense we shall merely have gained a respite, and our
descendants will find themselves under the necessity of marshalling
their power afresh for the siege of the Heartland. ... In other
words, we must settle this question between the Germans and the
Slavs and we must see to it that East Europe, like West Europe, is
divided into self-contained nations.*

Indeed, Mackinder's solution for peace in Europe and in the
world was the creation of what he called 'a tier of independent
States between Germany and Russia'. This creation of 'seven
independent States with a total of more than sixty million
people, traversed by railways linking them securely with one

* H. J. Mackinder: *Democratic Ideals and Reality* (London, 1919). The
Heartland is 'the entire Russian–Eurasian territory'.

another and having access through the Adriatic, Black and Baltic Seas with the ocean will be sufficient for ensuring that neither the Germans will cross eastwards nor the Russians advance westwards', if, apart from this territorial settlement the League of Nations, which at the time when Mackinder was writing was in the making, would 'have the right under international law of sending war fleets into the Black and Baltic Seas.'

In retrospect, we can now see that because this last and rather unexpected requirement remained unfulfilled, the entire security of the new Europe which, when it emerged from the peace treaties of 1919–21, was akin to that described by Mackinder, was compromised. Poland, Czechoslovakia, Hungary, Yugoslavia, Rumania, Bulgaria and Greece, fully sovereign national States, did indeed form a tier of independent States between Germany and Russia. The League of Nations had come into being and during its existence, for some twenty years, there was peace in Europe and the small States of the Continent enjoyed an unprecedented period of sovereignty. But when, after the world economic crisis, the fate of Europe was again decided by the contradictions and conflict of interests between the Great Powers, three of them now of the new totalitarian type (Soviet Russia, Fascist Italy and Nazi Germany), the League of Nations, which without supra-national organs such as a fleet, army or police force could not act as an international force, collapsed from within like a sand-castle. The League was one of the first victims of Hitler and Mussolini. Without it the 'tier' of independent Eastern European States rapidly disintegrated too. Left to themselves they engaged in a pathetic and selfish search for individual escape, running incoherently in a self-styled policy of individual neutralism, between the Great Powers: the democratic Governments of Britain and France, and Hitler, Mussolini and Stalin.

The crucial shortcoming in the Eastern European countries after the First World War was a lack of internal coherence and organization. Too weak individually to resist external pressures, their only chance of survival could have been found in their union, through some form of quasi-federal association, on the basis of which they could have opposed their multiplied common strength to the individual or combined challenges from the West and East. But from its first appearance on the world stage the 'tier' was badly split into two groups: the victorious, *status-quo*-minded ones: Poland, Czechoslovakia, Rumania and Yugoslavia, and the defeated, revisionist ones: Hungary and Bulgaria. France in the early twenties proceeded to build these States into a '*cordon sanitaire*' against Bolshevik Russia and also into her eastern flank against a resurgent Germany. Justified as this diplomatic design may have been, it nevertheless produced two unfortunate results: it caused new countries like Poland, Rumania and Czechoslovakia to centre their policies around diplomatic and military alliances with the Western Powers, leaving them too little time to concentrate on their own social and economic policies as well as their own union, with all the other Eastern European nations, into an independent 'tier' or bloc. It also aggravated the dissensions between them: the alliances and *ententes* which they forged between themselves were directed rather against the other two, Hungary and Bulgaria, than designed to form a new and genuine basis for some federal links. (Only in 1933 the Little Entente came nearer setting up some intergovernmental organs of consultation, but even this was a reaction against Hitler's coming to power.) The revisionist countries, Hungary and Bulgaria, soon became the clients of Fascist Italy, whose first diplomatic moves were designed to counter French hegemony on the Continent.

But even so, the democratic parties and statesmen and Governments of all these predominantly agrarian countries had enough historic common sense not to throw themselves into Hitler's arms when he made his bid for influence in Eastern Europe. He had to undermine them by creating in each of them Fascist parties linked to his secret police in order to impose his will and ultimately to occupy them. In each of these countries there was a strong, instinctive and traditional impulse towards some kind of union by which together they could form a Power of their own. But this was precisely what the Great Powers and especially the totalitarian Powers tried above all to prevent. The last instance of this was in 1947, after the Second World War, when, in circumstances which have already been analysed earlier in this survey, Communist Yugoslavia, Bulgaria, Rumania and Poland toyed with the idea of some federalization among themselves. They roused Russia's wrath to the point of precipitating Tito's exclusion from the Communist family, while the leaders of the other countries had to produce abject denials and apologies for ever having considered a project so fundamentally opposed to the interests of the present dominant Power.

In spite of the importance of Eastern Europe's own political problems, it is none the less necessary to regard it in the overall context of world-wide East–West relations. From the end of the war and up to the sixties these relations have taken the form of a struggle for influence throughout the world between two irreconcilable camps: the Communist bloc and the free world. The Communist bloc, considering itself in a state of immanent offensive against the 'capitalist-imperialist' Powers, tried to drive them out of every position on the world front by the means or combination of means most suitable to any area at any given moment: military, political, economic and ideological.

Since 1960 some of the crudest aspects of this struggle between the two rival groups have been attenuated and this development has greatly strengthened the hopes of all those who believed in the theory of 'convergence'. According to this theory, given time and patience, the ideological asperities between what is loosely called capitalism and what is emphatically described as communism will be reduced. As the two types of régime mellow together and observe each other without prejudice, both sides will discover that the similarities between them are greater than ideologically opposed interpretations make them appear. Industrialization and equalization of economic development have the same effect in different societies; the supreme responsibilities of the nuclear and space-exploring age bring the leaders of the various societies closer together; the rise to power and social hegemony of the same social groups – the technocrats and intellectuals – in both societies narrow the initial differences in outlook; the rising standard of living, universal although unequal, levels off the differences between classes of the same people and especially between peoples of different continents; finally, while capitalism corrects itself by accepting an increased amount of nationalization and state-control in its functioning, communism changes from within by accepting more and more the inevitable realities of free initiative, private ownership and incentives in its rigid structure.

Some vague notion of a universal 'socialism' acceptable to both Western and Eastern Europe is sometimes put forward; and perhaps the contacts between the Yugoslav Communist Party and the British Labour Party in the early fifties brought this idea closer. Finally, from a political point of view, the theory of 'convergence' is echoed by that of 'disengagement'. This is based on the idea that if the confrontation of the two opposite camps and of their outposts could be stopped in areas where the conflagration is most likely to start and if instead more pacified or neutralized zones could be created as buffers between the two opposed camps – all this could lead towards disarmament which in turn would be the beginning of a peaceful solution. Opposed to the theory of convergence is the view that the longer communism continues to exist in a more flexible and adaptable form, the stronger grow its roots and the sharper the difference between its ultimately ideological and totalitarian structure and that of the régimes founded on the basic economic and political freedoms.

In the context of Eastern Europe, however, two things are clear. On the one hand, for the twenty years with which this survey is concerned, the elements of convergence were overshadowed by the political conflict. On the other hand, whatever the variations introduced into the doctrine of communism, none of its spokesmen or leaders have publicly repudiated the final goal of world victory and its corollary: that throughout the world the Communist movement and the parties which form it advance with the same determination to 'bury' the free world as rang in Khrushchev's voice when he launched his famous slogan during his visit to the United States in 1958.

But both historically and politically Eastern Europe is a region with a special role. Historically, it was the region from which the two world wars sprang, as well as the Nazi–Soviet war. Politically, it stands out because the present unnatural division of the Continent is an obvious reality which strikes everyone; because the influence of Europe is more considerable than that of most of the other regions of the world and any change in its balance affects the centres of world politics directly; and because as a territorial area it is the main and the most likely potential battlefield, and therefore that part of the earth's surface where the accumulation of military power is, per square mile, highest, and where the 'escalation' could be more rapid than anywhere else.

As such, therefore, Eastern Europe is one of the first places, if not the first, in which a world war could start. But this does not mean that world peace can be won by solving the East European problem alone. It is on the contrary more true to say that the East European problem is bound up with two larger problems: the world-wide one of general disarmament; and that of European security. And the latter problem is from many points of view linked with and dependent on the German problem, which is the main obstacle to any European settlement.

The German problem conditions that of Eastern Europe in three respects. First, because the entire region is situated between the traditionally antagonistic Powers of Russia and Germany, its precarious political balance is substantially influenced by the relations between these two Powers. Secondly, because at the present juncture of history Germany is partitioned; one part is integrated in Western Europe and the Western world and the other maintained in the Communist bloc by massive Soviet forces and the Berlin Wall. This partition was initially the effect but is now the cause of the entire partition of Europe. It was an effect because the Soviet army could not have reached and occupied that zone of Germany had it not first reached and occupied the territories lying between it and the Russian frontiers. But it is now the cause, because in order to maintain Eastern Germany within its orbit, Soviet Russia needs the free passage across, and communications with, East Germany. And thirdly the German problem is relevant to

Eastern Europe as a whole because Soviet Russia wants not only to maintain Eastern Germany within her zone of domination in Europe but to make of it a viable Communist State, which is, from every point of view, an unattainable proposition.

The Berlin Wall is the terrible proof of the fact that if they were not sealed off by such primitive and artificial means the people, to paraphrase a saying of Bert Brecht, would dissolve before the State. Economically, too, East Germany cannot be maintained in existence except by strong ties with Soviet Russia and the Eastern European countries. East Germany remains thus the greatest obstacle in the 'Communist commonwealth' to any ideas of further liberalization which might conceivably be acceptable to the majority of the other people's republics. It has also become the most vociferous promoter of the idea of the close economic integration of the entire region, under the auspices of COMECON, into a quasi-federal Common-Market-type political and economic unit. This of course is an old Soviet hope which would enable Russia to recover by the back door greater power of control over the economies of the people's democracies, much of which she lost after Stalin's death. But while the German Democratic Republic sees in such a policy the best way to drown its perennial economic bankruptcy in the combined resources of all the other countries, the latter are aware of the ultimate danger of being once more drawn into Soviet Russia's belly. This led, in 1963, to the great Rumanian–East German–Russian conflict about the transformation of COMECON into a supra-national authority in which the Rumanians managed to defeat the whole plan.

The political importance of Eastern Europe is as relatively high today as it was during the first and fourth decades of the twentieth century when two world wars and the Nazi–Soviet war sprang from the contest of wills between the world Powers over it. But the fact is that Eastern Europe is no longer today the only fortified region in the world where the opposing Powers face each other with the clear determination that any move on either side should be countered at any cost. Although the line dividing Eastern and Western Europe still undoubtedly remains one of the world's regions most obviously fraught with danger, there are now in this global encounter other such fortified regions of perpetual alert; moreover, such mobility has been achieved that any place in the world can, by rapid escalation, become the first theatre of operations whence war would quickly take its natural course towards the nuclear duel over the centres of power.

The nuclear and missile warfare has outdated all classic military doctrine and strategy. Distances have been annihilated; the first casualties of the new outlook were the defensive 'lines' or 'buffers'. The new war will be fought in the air and over the centres, not on the land or on the borders of the main belligerents. At the same time, territorial distances will be overrun at the increased speed of contemporary and future aircraft, and vehicles. Stalin had altogether three defensive lines. The first and original Stalin line, with some kind of Maginot fortifications and with deep defensive zones and anti-tank obstacles, ran before 1939 along the general line Uman–Kiev–Vitebsk–Staraya Russia. The occupation in 1939–40 of the Baltic States, parts of Eastern Poland, Bessarabia and northern Bukovina transferred the first line of defence to these newly acquired 'marches'. Yet the German panzers overran these territories in a matter of hours. The third Stalin line, as he consolidated it after the Second World War, was what seemed to be the deep and comfortable stretch of the whole of Eastern Europe which, as the crow flies, is about five hundred miles. This belt combined with the forces and the raw materials which can be drawn from these rich and populated countries seemed to Stalin and his advisers to form the best defence Russia had ever attained in her military history – not to speak of its enormous importance as a thrust into the heart of Europe and of Germany, which opened the way for direct Soviet action in many other parts of Europe.

Hence for the first time Eastern Europe does not appear as the almost inevitable arena for an East–West war. In this sense it can be said that the whole of Eastern Europe, with its distances, populations, bases and fortifications, represents an even less effective obstacle for the contemporary and for the future methods of transport than was the stretch formed by the

Baltic States, Eastern Poland and Bessarabia against the advance of the German forces in 1941. And yet the strategic (that is both offensive and defensive) point of view played and plays an overwhelming role among the reasons which moved Stalin and his successors to erect and to try to maintain in existence the Russian post-Second World War empire in Eastern Europe, in spite of the foreseeable risks and disadvantages.

Bibliography

Berlin, Isaiah: *Karl Marx*, London, 1960.

Brzezinski, Zbigniew: *The Soviet Bloc, Unity and Conflict*, New York, 1963.

Carew Hunt, R. N.: *The Theory and Practice of Communism*, London, 1960.

Crankshaw, Edward: *The New Cold War, Moscow* v. *Pekin*, London, 1963; *Krushchev's Russia*, London, 1962.

Dallin, Alexander: *Diversity in International Communism: A Documentary Record, 1961–63*, New York, 1963.

Dedijer, Vladimir: *Tito*, London, 1953.

Djilas, Milovan: *The New Class*, London, 1957.

Fischer Galati, Stephen: *Eastern Europe in the Sixties*, New York, 1963.

Griffith, William: *Albania and the Sino-Soviet Rift*, M.I.T., 1963.

Hiscocks, Richard: *Poland, Bridge for the Abyss?*, London, 1963.

Ionescu, Ghita: *Communism in Rumania*, London, 1963.

Labedz, Leo: *Revisionism*, London, 1962.

Macartney, C. A.: *October 15, History of Modern Hungary*, London, 1956.

Nagy Imre: *On Communism*, London, 1957.

Royal Institute of International Affairs: Survey of International Affairs, 1939–46: *America, Britain and Russia: Their Co-operation and Conflict, 1941–46*, by W. H. McNeil, 1953; 'Eastern Europe' by Martin Wright in *World in March 1939*, 1952.

Schapiro, Leonard: *The Origin of the Communist Autocracy*, London, 1955; *The Communist Party of the Soviet Union*, London, 1960.

Seton-Watson, G. H. N.: *Eastern Europe between the Wars, 1918–41*, London, 1946; *The East European Revolution*, London, 1951; *The Pattern of Communist Revolutions*, London, 1951.

Taborski, E.: *Communism in Czechoslovakia*, London, 1961.

Zinner, Paul: *National Communism and Popular Revolt in Eastern Europe: a Selection of Documents on Events in Poland and Hungary, Feb.-Nov. 1956*, New York, 1956.